The
NLP Trainer Training
Manual

Peter Freeth

CGW
PUBLISHING

2017

The NLP Trainer Training Manual

Peter Freeth

First Edition: April 2017

ISBN 978-1-9082932-8-2

Published by:

CGW Publishing
B 1502
PO Box 15113
Birmingham
B2 2NJ
United Kingdom

www.cgwpublishing.com

mail@cgwpublishing.com

For information about NLP training programs, visit:

www.nenlp.com

www.geniuslearning.co.uk

Contents

Exercises

[1] NLP Trainer

If you're reading this now then you are most likely quite some way along your NLP learning journey, and I am delighted that you have made it this far. I've been waiting for you.

If you are not reading this now then something has gone horribly wrong. I suggest switching yourself off and back on again.

That's actually a pretty good summary of the process of learning. Read something. Stop reading it. Switch off and back on. Repeat. Nice and simple. However, humans do like to complicate things.

Learning is very easy because you are a learning machine. Like Neo in the film The Matrix, you can assimilate new information into your brain remarkably quickly and efficiently, and then you can forget most of that just as quickly if it's not relevant to you.

As a NLP Trainer, you will learn how to shape and guide this natural process. Learning NLP is not like learning maths or history. Long division presents no challenge to the ego. The factors which led to the First World War do not require the learner to push through any personal barriers. Of course, exam anxiety plays a part in the student's success, but that's not what we're talking about here. The very process of learning NLP changes the student, and that change creates friction and resistance. If you, the Trainer, cannot manage that, your learners will only ever skim the surface. You will sign certificates, knowing in your heart that you are unleashing ineffective, inexperienced and substandard Practitioners and Master Practitioners onto the world. Those students aren't painting fences and driving buses, they are engaging with clients of their own through coaching, counselling, even therapy. You have a responsibility to those clients because you are putting your name on the certificate of the people who they are entrusting their lives to.

After all, if you were training bus drivers, you would consider passenger safety, wouldn't you? Wouldn't you?

Being a NLP Trainer is more than a set of skills or a certificate, it is a responsibility both to your students and to their friends, families, colleagues and clients.

If you're not ready to accept that responsibility then it is unlikely that you will meet the certification criteria for a NLP trainer. If you are ready then let's get started.

People describe NLP in different ways; a study of excellence, a model of human communication and behaviour or a toolkit for personal change are ones you may have heard. Some NLP trainers even present NLP as a panacea for all ills; it can give you confidence, wealth, contentment, good health and more. Because of this, NLP has earned a reputation from some critics for being a hyped up, pseudo-scientific cult that tries to pass itself off as a branch of psychology, or neuro-science, or psychiatry, depending on which website you're looking at.

At the heart of NLP is a set of linguistic tools for understanding the intuitive mindset and behaviour of excellence in any field.

At this Trainer level of NLP Training, we actually have to achieve two things. Firstly, we need to develop a set of skills which are broader than those explored at the Practitioner and Master Practitioner levels. Secondly, we must develop an understanding of the process of learning itself. We must not just be teachers of knowledge, we must be guides on the journey itself.

You see, when we train NLP, we're not just teaching facts and figures like the wives of Henry the Eighth or how to do simultaneous equations. We are guiding our students through a process of personal change. This is very prominent at Practitioner level, where the primary purpose of the training is, through learning the techniques of NLP, to give the student a first hand experience of change.

At Master Practitioner level, we want out students to see the world in a fundamentally different way, to see through the facade presented by people and see the patterns and programs behind their language and behaviour. To do this, the student must acknowledge their own facade, their own patterns and programs.

What, then, are we aiming for at Trainer level?

By following the same logic, if we are to teach others how to teach, we must first learn how to learn. NLP Trainer Training therefore works at two levels – superficially developing the skills to train NLP and its techniques, but at a deeper level, you must overcome your own barriers and prejudices to learning so that you can more clearly see those of your students. To accept learning in all of its forms requires you to accept that you are not yet complete, that there is more to learn than you already know. Learning changes your world view, and you along with it.

I'm privileged that you are joining me for this part of your journey, and I hope that you enjoy exploring and learning NLP as much as I do.

[2] What's the Point?

What is the point, the purpose of your NLP training, or of any kind of training for that matter?

You went to school, I presume. What was that all about? Did you learn anything useful? Did it prepare you for the world of work? Have you learned more in, or out of school?

Some people say, "I'm always learning". Well, obviously. If you're alive, then your senses are representing information from the outside world. Your brain is comparing that information, extracting differences and storing those differences away for future reference. We call this process 'learning' so, as long as you're alive, you're learning. It's a defining characteristic of intelligent life, here on Earth at least. Whether we're talking about humans, dogs, dolphins, elephants, raccoons, apes, crows or any of the animals that are now regarded as having 'near human intelligence', learning is the very basis of adaptation. There's no point surviving a life-threatening incident, only to get caught out in the same way the next day. If there's a lion hiding behind that tree, it might be there tomorrow too.

Learning, as a description of our ongoing sensory experience, is therefore something that can take place in any or all of our sensory experience. We have at least 21 senses, so that's a lot of data to learn from.

Whoa! Aren't there 5 senses, with submodalities? No. The concept of submodalities is purely a NLP construction, there is no evidence for them. They are fabrications, figments of the imagination to explain the distortions that we make in order to choose the meaning of our memories.

The sensory pathways and receptors can be extremely tiny, so scientists are discovering new ones regularly. Just in the past few months, scientists have finally found what gives certain animals a sense of direction - a protein molecule which orients along magnetic field lines. Even more recently, scientists have discovered a sixth sense of taste in humans – starch.

We don't need to invent concepts to explain our sensory experiences when our own physical capabilities are so amazing.

Sight	Colour – light in the frequency range 390 to 750 nm, a good match for reflected sunlight. Usually Red, Green and Blue, some people don't have a Green receptor, some people have an additional Yellow receptor. The cone cells are tubes so small that they interfere with light at different frequencies and create vibrations.
Sight	Brightness, also vital in edge detection and therefore focus, with a resolution of one arc minute, equivalent to a line 0.3mm wide held at arm's length.
Sweet	Get energy now.
Starch	Get energy tomorrow.
Umami	Get energy this week.
Sour	It's gone off, don't eat it.
Bitter	It's poisonous, don't eat it.
Salt	It's sea water, don't drink it.

Touch	Multipoint resolution of between 2mm and 45mm and depth of 75nm.
Pressure	I can't take this pressure, oh!
Heat	Up to 45°C with a resolution of 0.02°C.
Cold	Down to 5°C with a resolution of 0.02°C.
Nociception	Outside of 5 to 45°C we feel heat or cold as pain.
Itch	Detects creepy-crawlies.
Sound	The shape of your ear canal allows hairs to resonate at different frequencies in the range of 20Hz to 20kHz which are then 'reassembled' by your brain. The quietest sounds you can hear are between -5dB and +5dB, and the cells attached to those hairs can detect movement smaller than the size of an atom. Your ears use an active feedback system to amplify some sounds.
Smell	Probably multiple senses too. Some people can't smell skunks. About 50 molecules are required to detect a smell.
Proprioception	Feedback from your muscles that helps you to locate your limbs and weigh things in your hands.
Tension	In the lungs, bladder, stomach and intestine. Also detect the dilation of blood vessels.

Equilibrioception	Balance, using both fluid-filled tubes and hairs weighted with calcium carbonite crystals.
Chemoreceptors	Detect hormones and toxins in the blood.
Thirst	Some people think they're hungry when they're actually thirsty.
Hunger	Feed me, Seymour.
Magnetoception	Mole rats have tiny particles of iron in receptor cells. Birds, primates and dogs have Cryptochromes in their retinas.
Elestroreception	Some sea animals have Ampullae of Lorenzini which detect electrical fields.

The traditional "five senses" model that NLP's 'VAKOG+submodalities' model is based on is credited to Aristotle, who lived from 384 BC to 322 BC. He also thought that the function of the brain was to provide cooling for the blood.

Learning creates change, and it is the journey of learning which is important, not the facts.

During my time in the corporate world, I often worked for managers who had no respect for learning, who perceived no value in time spent in training.

Rather than attending a day's training, they would want to read the accompanying presentation slides. Worse, they would want a one page summary of what would be covered in the training, a list of facts, devoid of any context. They would look through the facts, decide that they already knew 'all that' and dismiss the training as a waste of time.

Training was not my job at that time, yet I still knew that the value of learning is in the change in the learner's perception, not in the facts that they can recall, and that change cannot come from reading a list of facts.

Facts are the output of the learning process, not the input.

Many years ago, I worked on a project for gifted and talented children where, over a 2 week period, a group of children would devise, design, write, build and perform a stage production with support from a team of adults.

After the performance, the children were given feedback forms to complete. One of the questions was, "What did you learn?" and a girl, who had been particularly 'difficult' at the start of the course wrote, "I learned how to put on a play". When I asked her, "What else did you learn?" she didn't understand.

"Well, did you learn anything that was nothing to do with putting on a play?"

Without hesitation, she said, "Oh yes! I learned to be more tolerant of other people."

I asked, "How do you know that you learned that?"

Her reply was wonderful. "Because I haven't bitten anyone."

What, then, is the point? Perhaps that we humans are always learning, but we don't necessarily know *what* we're learning until we have an opportunity to step back and reflect and comment on what we're learning, and we can only do that at the end of the process. "What have you learned so far?" is perhaps not a useful question. Learning is something complete, something that can only be whole.

Our studies of learning give us new insights which make learning more effective. We know that reciting the wives of King Henry VIII is utterly pointless. We know that learning the theory of swimming whilst sitting at a school desk won't save your life. What we don't know is if e-learning and bite-sized learning and v-learning and mobile learning are just as ineffective. If we could download knowledge directly into our brains like in The Matrix, then we wouldn't need to go to school. Or would we? Would the purpose of school then change? Like it or not, our time at school taught us a great deal, but not about chemistry or history. Our school years set us up for many future experiences, and as wonderful and multisensory and multidisciplinary our schools are today, we still manage to teach our kids a bunch of stuff that they will never need to know until, one day, they too are yelling at the TV screen during their favourite quiz show.

In each generation, we do our best to pass on our knowledge to make life easier and more rewarding for the next. And the harder we work to improve the learning process, the more we miss the simplest truth of all. We cannot not learn. Yet learning for the purpose of passing exams is different to learning for the purpose of survival. As a NLP Trainer you must take all of this into account if you are to create truly memorable experiences for your learners.

3 What is Learning?

Before we get too wrapped up in how wonderful NLP is, we should take a step back and consider the bigger question – what is 'learning'? What does it mean, 'to learn'?

3.1.1.1   What is learning?

We could explore this with a few questions. Take some time to come up with your own answers, then discuss this in small groups, then present your conclusions from your small groups to the entire group.

What have you learned during your life?

What have you learned since this morning?

What are you intending to learn for the rest of today?

You may notice that over short periods of time you tend to recall facts or events, whilst over longer periods of time you tend to give more generalised examples of learning. Why is this?

Can you really set out to learn something?

Or do you need a motive, a reason, a trigger for learning?

Looking back over your life, what lessons have been hard to learn?

What made those lessons hard to learn?

Would you describe your experiences at school as 'learning'?

Why?

How do you sometimes make learning difficult for yourself?

How can you therefore make learning easy for yourself?

And how can you use this to make learning easier for others?

And with all of this in mind, what is learning?

Let's imagine that learning is the process of acquiring, assimilating, simplifying and generalising our experiences in life for the purpose of increasing our opportunities for surviving future events.

If that is true, then we would tend to learn things that would confer some kind of survival advantage. Our minds have adapted very well to this modern way of living, so consider all of the faces you recognise, the songs you can sing, the streets you could navigate to, the books and films you could quote from and the rich sensory experiences that you can describe.

Now imagine that you had been born into a remote tribe in the rainforest. At most, you will meet 100 people during your entire lifetime, you will stay within a few miles of where you were born and your experiences of life will be entirely constrained by that environment. And yet, with that comparatively limited lifestyle, you will be equipped with exactly the same brain, with exactly the same learning capabilities. What would you use it for?

Simply, you would remember every leaf so that you could know in an instant if an animal had used a path through the forest. You would remember every star, and use its position to navigate in complete darkness. You would know every story of every moment of the lives of your friends, family and ancestors. You would know every call of every bird, and you would know every flower, leaf and berry and its purpose.

You would know as much as you know now.

Just take a moment to imagine that.

[4] Modelling Learners

You have probably been on a motion simulator at a funfair. It might have featured a roller-coaster ride, or a runaway train, or a jet fighter performing aerobatics. The machine itself is just a combination of two things; a video, taking from the participant's eye view, and a 'motion platform' that shakes you about in time with the movie.

However enjoyable these rides may be, you're very unlikely to believe that you actually were on a real roller-coaster. However, what is most fascinating about these machines is that they can simulate so many different activities. The operator just puts in a different DVD and a spaceship is transformed into an airboat, skimming over Florida's Everglades. The simulation is good enough for most people to suspend reality just long enough to enjoy the ride.

Professional flight simulators are something quite different. They take an actual cockpit from the aircraft in question and place it within the motion platform. Incredibly complex and detailed graphics simulate any airport, complete with the right aircraft and vehicles on the ground, weather, terrain and feedback through the aircraft's cockpit displays. These simulators are so accurate that when a pilot crashes one, the stress is as severe as if the aircraft were real, and time in a simulator is equivalent to time in the air, as far as licensing is concerned.

After half an hour in a flight simulator, you would definitely be forgiven for forgetting that you were never more than thirty feet from the ground.

Meteorologists spend much of their time gathering data from weather stations. On top of buildings, at airports and out on remote hillsides, monitoring stations collect data on wind speed and direction, rainfall, temperature and humidity. Why are they so interested in collecting such useless data? Is it just so that they can tell us that it's been the wettest July since 1903?

No. The reason that they collect this data is so that they can constantly refine and update their weather models. By comparing their simulations to actual conditions, they can increase their confidence in their predictions. The scientist Nikola Tesla was said to construct mental models that he ran alongside his physical experiments. He would lock his experiments in a room and after many days or even months, discover that the physical experiment matched his mental simulation perfectly.

This shouldn't be surprising, though, because you can do exactly the same thing. You can put some bread under the grill and go into another room. The phone rings, you end up chatting, you forget about the toast and when you start to smell smoke, you instantly know what you're going to find under the grill. How surprised would you be if you *didn't* find two smouldering squares of charcoal?

And when you return to a favourite restaurant or holiday destination, how do you feel when it's not how you remembered it?

Sometimes, you criticise yourself. It might be when you feel you have made an obvious mistake, or it might be when you knew you should have listened to your intuition but didn't.

One of the first things that most people learn in NLP training is how to listen to and modify their internal dialogue. You learn to hear the sound of your father or mother chastising you and modify it to be a carton character or newsreader, with the effect that you don't feel so bad about the mistake you made.

This doesn't work in the real world. If you are cornered in a dark alley by a knife wielding thug, imagining him with a clown's nose might alleviate the tension but it doesn't change the fact that he's after your money.

We build simulations that mirror reality so that we can predict what will happen in reality and take action to achieve our goals and avoid danger.

Imagine that someone throws a snowball at you. Given enough time, you can intuitively compute the snowball's flight path and move your head out of the way, just in time. This is an incredibly complex thing to be able to do, and it cannot be achieved by reacting, because by the time you react, the snowball is no longer where it was when you saw it.

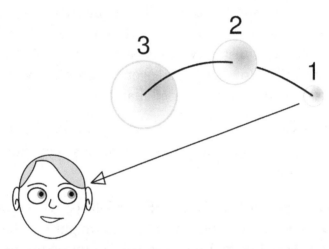

When the snowball is in position 1, the light reflected from it arrives at your eyes almost instantly, but the signal from your retinas takes a much longer period of time to reach your brain, by which time the snowball, which is moving at a fairly constant speed, is in position 2. Your brain takes time to process the visual information, compute the snowball's path, determine in which direction to move to avoid the snowball and begin signalling to your muscles through your motor cortex, by which time the snowball is in position 3.

By the time your muscles begin to respond, the snowball is now in this position:

After you have recovered, you will probably feel a little silly that you saw the snowball but couldn't get out of the way fast enough to avoid it. No matter how good your reactions are, you can never overcome this signal delay.

When you think about the computation required to recognise a fast moving object as an incoming icy missile, determine its path, calculate avoiding action and then translate that action into specific muscle movements, it's a wonder that you get to see the snowball at all.

Having a good reaction time simply means that you don't have to think about what to do for as long, but there is nothing that you can do about that signal delay. By the time you are processing the image of the snowball, it has already moved further along its flight path, and by the time your muscles begin contracting, it has moved further still.

At a very early age, you learned to simulate the laws of motion. Newton wrote them out in plain English for other people to understand, and from those laws we can now throw snowballs with some degree of accuracy, and we can also launch a spaceship with three men on board, land it on the moon and return it to Earth with only a few minutes of fuel to spare.

If you have read The NLP Practitioner Manual, you may recall that in 2005, NASA launched a probe called Deep Impact that, seven months later, crashed into the "Tempel 1" comet. The comet is essentially a lump of ice, 4 miles across and travelling at about 23,000 mph. The probe was about the size of a washing machine.

NASA's analogy is that the probe hitting the comet is like a pebble hitting a truck. A pebble that you threw seven months ago.

Just imagine that for a moment. You look through a telescope and see a comet, millions of miles away. You observe it every day and, accounting for the time it takes the light reflected from the comet to reach your telescope, you calculate the comet's path, using equations that were developed over 300 years ago in 1687. The Wright brothers didn't achieve sustained, heavier than air flight until more than 200 years later in 1903. Yet you can calculate the path of the comet with such confidence that you can take something the size of a washing machine, place it on top of a very large firework, light the blue touch paper and launch it out beyond Earth's atmosphere where it just floats along at its own pace, obeying Newton's first law of motion until, seven months later, the paths of the comet and the probe intersect.

A certain genre of film associated with martial arts often shows the hero shooting an arrow and knocking an enemy's arrow out of the air. It's utterly implausible, but no less impossible, technically, than a military anti-missile system that can hit something the size of a baguette travelling at 2,600 mph.

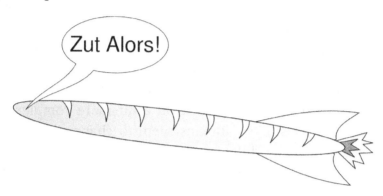

The only difference between the film and reality is that computers are much better at computing flight paths, quickly, than most humans are.

Remember, the purpose of a simulation is to be able to predict the future.

When people act inappropriately, or they act in a certain way because of the reaction that they hope to get, they are trying to control future events. If I want to open a door, I can predict the amount of force with which to push or pull it. I try to control the future behaviour of the door in order to achieve an outcome.

A child learns to control future events by asking for more pocket money when Daddy's watching the football, or Mummy's on the phone. But parents can "wise up" to these early attempts at manipulation, and the child has to revise its simulations.

We cannot ever get away from simulations because they literally make us who we are. However, what we can seek to do is narrow the gap between our simulations and reality, just like the meteorologists do, and this is the goal of NLP.

Creating a simulation of an inanimate object, moving within the consistent and predictable 'laws' of physics isn't that difficult. We know this because we can program computers to make predictions based on the constants that govern the motion of objects, gravity, the behaviour of gases as their temperature changes and so on. But humans are quite different; their behaviour based on a far more complex set of rules and constants. Humans seem to change over time, they seem to make different choices in the same situation from one day to the next and they adapt to changes in the external environment.

Philosophers have, over many thousands of years, attempted to understand human behaviour, coming up with various theories to define this experience that we call "reality". Yet, intuitively, we have each mastered the ability to predict the complexities of "human nature". You walk into a bar to meet a friend and correctly order a drink for them, even when it's not what they normally have. A parent preempts their child's behaviour and prevents an embarrassing situation at a restaurant. You weigh up a dilemma and the mentor on your shoulder gives you exactly the advice that they would offer if they were sitting in front of you.

I'm sure you've had this latter experience. Your hand reaches for the chocolate and a voice in the back of your head reminds you of the promise you made to yourself. Whose voice is it? We build simulations of people close to us that are so lifelike that they often seem to take on a life of their own, giving direction, advice and criticism as if the person was there in the room with you.

Children need to acquire their parents' experiences in order to stay safe. They need to learn boundaries and in order to operate independently as responsible adults, they need to live by those rules without they parent watching over their every move. But we often inherit more rules from our parents than we would like, and it can be difficult for some people to separate the useful rules from those which have become outdated.

One of the aspects of mental simulation that is most often cited in the self-help world is mental rehearsal. The idea is that by running through a scenario in your mind, you can develop the same level of skill as if you were really practising it. Taken to extremes, some celebrity self-help gurus talk about the "law" of attraction, which means that by harbouring positive thoughts, you can 'manifest' wealth and happiness into your life. Sadly, such claims discredit the underlying science which is regularly used by athletes when they rehearse for races. They can't control what their opponents will do on the day, but they can rehearse the track in their minds until every twist and turn is 'second nature' to them.

What is the reality of mental rehearsal? Does it simply build a memory of a task, or does it affect the body too? When people are asked to imagine a task while in a MRI scanner, the results show that many brain areas are engaged just as they would be in the physical performance of that task. But surely, this doesn't affect someone's muscles. How could it? Yet research conducted by Alvaro Pascual-Leone indicates that practice not only reinforces a person's memory of a task, it also enlarges the brain's motor area for the muscles that control that task. More output neurons means stronger muscles and better muscle control. Pascual-Leone used a technology called TMS (Transcranial Magentic Stimulation) to map brain activity in great detail. In a study of people learning to play the piano, he compared people practising at a real keyboard with people who were simply *imagining* playing. After five days, the 'mental' players required only a two hour live practice session to acquire the same level of skill as the people who had practised on a real keyboard.

In another study, Drs Yue and Cole compared a group of people undertaking physical exercise with a group who just imagined exercising. At the end of the four week study, the people who had physically exercised had increased their muscle strength by 30%. Surprisingly, the people who had only *imagined* the same exercise increased their muscle strength by 22%.

We mustn't get carried away with such news; while mental rehearsal can strengthen the brain's connections to muscles, the muscles themselves don't change, and you certainly won't 'think yourself thin'. However, when learning fine motor tasks such as are involved in sports or music, mental rehearsal clearly benefits the learning process.

In 2000, I worked as a teacher for a 'gifted and talented' project, running weekend and holiday courses for young children. On one course, a number of the children said that they wanted to be able to use a computer keyboard more quickly, so I tried an experiment. Their starting level of ability was to type with the index finger of their dominant hand, with a few seconds delay between key presses while they searched around the keyboard for the key they wanted. I theorised that, once they had found a letter, they didn't forget where it was. The reason that they searched for each letter was that they only *thought* they didn't know which letters were in which location, when at some unconscious level, they intuitively knew. In fact, young children can easily acquire 'procedural knowledge', enabling them to learn a task, but only when their brains have further developed can they articulate that knowledge. So intuitively knowing the location of a letter on a keyboard but not being able to translate that into the sound or word would probably make sense.

I gave the children a series of very simple, repetitive tasks to perform. First, I had them typing rows and rows of letters in the order that they appear on the keyboard; QWERTY... After a few minutes, the children's' typing got faster and settled into a comfortable rhythm, so I changed the task to typing the letters in alphabetical order; ABCDE... Again, their typing was slow at first but soon accelerated and settled into a rhythm. I then changed the task to 'the quick brown fox...' and this time, as they practised typing, I distracted them by saying the alphabet backwards, counting and so on. What happened was quite remarkable; the more I distracted them, the faster they could type.

I then let them rest, and then had them imagine typing, and asked them to imagine themselves in different scenarios; at school, at home, with friends, typing letters, emails, and perhaps most importantly, receiving positive comments, praise and supportive feedback. Finally, I had them physically practice again. All of the children, a group of about 15, showed a marked increase in the speed and accuracy of their typing and, perhaps most importantly, their confidence that they *could* type.

Clearly, the more accurate and challenging the mental simulations we can build, the more we can achieve the ultimate goal of all self-help gurus; *to fulfil our potential.*

4.1 Brainy People

You are a very brainy person. In fact, we could even go so far as to say that you are one big brain. Every part of your body has evolved to serve the needs of your brain. Your senses gather external information and your muscles enable your brain to modify external events so that your sensory experience aligns with your desires.

Imagine, for a moment, a drink. Something that you want, perhaps a cup of tea or coffee. As you imagine it, you know exactly what to do in order to get it. By conjuring up that mental simulation, your entire neurology and physiology can spring into action to close the gap between desire and reality.

Most NLP books and training programs contain some descriptions of neurology and brain organisation. Even now, trainers are still talking about the triune brain or left/right brain function. These models are incredibly out of date, and fundamentally wrong.

The problem with NLP trainers who talk about neurology is that they are regurgitating knowledge that is at least forty years old, and of course they are largely regurgitating a rather one sided account of that knowledge which has more to do with NLP's early brand image than any real science.

I don't want you thinking that you only get upset because your amygdala takes over, or that your ancient reptilian brain is where all of your base desires live. This model of brain function is closer to the Victorian art of phrenology than to any modern understanding of brain science, even though it is still being taught on self-styled accelerated learning courses. By the way, why does it take three days to learn about accelerated learning? And why is there a book entitled, "Speed reading in a week". Shouldn't that be "Speed reading in five minutes"?

Even twenty years ago, a theory of 'holographic' brain function was emerging, where functions are spread across the brain rather than localised in particular areas. Even those localised areas are named, not after any understanding of their function, but after the person who first dissected them or the animal that they remind someone of. Your hippocampus is so named because it looks a bit like a seahorse. I suppose we should think our selves lucky that our neural structures are not shaped like anything more embarrassing.

We cannot figure out how the mind works by dissecting it, however there is another approach that we can learn from, and that is the approach taken by the people who are trying not to figure out how the brain *works* but to reproduce what it *does*.

Artificial Intelligence is one goal of computer research, however there seems to be some disagreement over what intelligence is, even though we can be fairly certain what the 'artificial' part refers to. Or can we? Robots have been built that use cells from rat brains to make navigational decisions, and electronic components have been inserted into peoples' bodies, and I'm not just talking about the assistant at the local electrical retailer who told me that they couldn't replace the mobile phone that I bought last week because it's already obsolete. No, I'm talking about people who have had artificial retinas and ear drums wired into their brains.

One of the most interesting people in this field of research is Steve Grand, who set out to build an artificial orang-utan called Lucy. His goal was to have Lucy point at a banana.

Now, this in itself is a very simple task. We can easily program a computer to recognise the characteristic shape and colour of a banana, under controlled conditions, and we can easily have that computer control a robotic arm to 'point' at that banana. You might have a digital camera that has 'face recognition' so that the camera can focus on the nearest face, even if it isn't centred in the frame. But that does not make your camera intelligent, it merely emulates one tiny aspect of your abilities, and that idea is central to the way that Steve Grand is approaching the problem. He built Lucy 'from the ground up', from first principles. Rather than building a robot to *do* something, such as paint a car or mow your lawn, he built Lucy to emulate the way that our brains are wired up, and in doing so, he figured out some very interesting functions that relate to our simulation theory of mind.

Since Steve Grand isn't terribly interested in NLP[1], and since most neuroscience authors probably aren't interested in Steve's attempts to build a mechanical monkey in his garage, it falls to us to bridge the gap between these two fascinating and complementary areas of research.

----

1   I asked him, he had never heard of it. Nice chap though.

For a long time, there has been a theory of brain function that represents the brain as a number of discrete functional areas. Visual processing here, right index finger there, sense of self awareness down in that corner. This model essentially developed from the study of one man, Phineas Gage, who we'll discuss later on. In short, he suffered a serious brain injury but survived, minus some aspects of his personality. This demonstrated that the bits of mental facility that he lost were resident in the bits of brain that were blown out of the top of his head by a large metal rod, and fitted very nicely with the observation that the rest of the human body is also made up of clearly delineated functional areas called organs.

However, as medical science has progressed, we no longer need to remove parts of the brain in order to deduce function, we can watch the brain in action in real time by giving people tasks and observing which parts of their brain draw more oxygen from blood flow, indicating increased activity and therefore functional significance.

I should point out that the latest neurological old wives' tale that is doing the rounds is that when you connect an EEG machine to a strawberry jelly, it shows the same signs of consciousness as are observed in the human brain. Therefore, to deduce brain function by observing brain operation is misleading at best. By the way, I cannot find any evidence of this supposed research, and it seems likely that it's an urban myth, like the early experiments into subliminal messaging which are often the subject of discussion on NLP training courses. By the time you read this, it will probably be 'common knowledge' that strawberry jelly is sentient, according to the neurologists whose statistical analysis of random electrical activity leaves them clutching at straws in an effort to prove that they can determine a person's thoughts from the electrical activity in their brains. You can mock them now, but when the fruit trifles move in and take all our women and jobs, you'll be laughing on the other side of your face.

Using other brain imaging methods, scientists have been able to see what a person is seeing. Kind of. "Using functional Magnetic Resonance Imaging (fMRI) and computational models, UC Berkeley researchers have succeeded in decoding and reconstructing people's dynamic visual experiences – in this case, watching Hollywood movie trailers."[2]

The technique didn't really show people's mental images, of course. It reconstructed something based on brain activity that the researchers thought was a bit like something they'd already seen. You've probably done something similar during your Practitioner training where you calibrated which memory a person was recalling by watching their facial expressions. During sales training, I sometimes get people to recall good and bad customers and then notice how this unconsciously affects their behaviour. The point is, if you have a point of reference then yes, you can figure out what someone is thinking. But from scratch, with a new subject, to see what they're thinking? We're way off that. It would be like an alien, looking at the tracks on a CD and reconstructing the music. A few more steps are required to figure out the code.

We now know that the brain is made up, not of functional organs, but of layers. Every sensory nerve ending in your body arrives, through your brain stem, into a primary input area, and every motor nerve leaves your brain through a primary output area.

---

2   news.berkeley.edu/2011/09/22/brain-movies

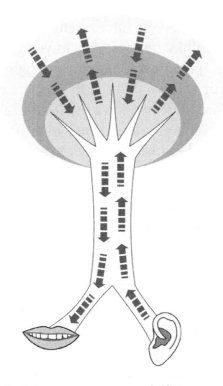

In that regard, humans are no different, neurologically, from any other animal; from earthworms to orang-utans. The key difference between ourselves and other animals is not the number of brain cells that we have, nor the number of chromosomes in our DNA; it is the number of processing steps that a signal goes through in between reception and action. Each of these processing steps could introduce an extra layer of finesse or detail into the overall decision process.

When a shadow passes over a frog, it dives for cover. It doesn't differentiate between a kestrel and a pigeon, as it simply reacts to a pattern of changing light levels. This means that a frog can react much faster than a human because there are fewer layers of processing in between 'shadow' and 'jump'. Similarly, if you have ever tried to swat a fly, you'll know that they excel at moving out of the way, just when you think you have them cornered. This isn't because the fly 'thinks' any faster than you do, it's simply to do with those previously mentioned signal delays. An external observer will see that the fly has already moved out of the way before your hand is anywhere near it, thanks to its short reception to action delay, and you're unable to adjust your action because you don't even know that the fly has moved. When you swat a fly with a rolled up newspaper, it's smaller than your hand but it's also moving a lot faster, and as long as you attack the fly from the same direction as it is flying towards, the result will be bad news for the fly.

Whilst frogs and flies can react faster than humans, they lack our versatility, and most importantly they lack our ability to understand and predict possible future events. If a predator approached you, you would have a number of choices available; freeze, run, grab a stick, try to distract it or even negotiate with it if the predator in question is a sales assistant in a furniture store. This versatility requires complex computational power, and that comes at the expense of raw speed.

Probably the most recognisable part of the human brain is the cortex, which is essentially a folded sheet of nerve tissue wrapped around the central parts of the brain. It's as if those original parts grew more and more layers, so those layers became folded in order to pack them inside your skull, much like a folded umbrella manages to pack a large surface area into an apparently small volume.

At the centre of all of this is a structure called the Superior Colliculus, through which all incoming and outgoing nerve connections are routed. One important observation which reinforces the theories that I'm covering here is that the more complex the behavioural response, the further into the cortex are the connections that drive that behaviour.

For example, fundamental behaviours such as breathing and regulating a heart beat are driven from within the brain stem itself. Our version of the frog's "Leg it!" response is called our 'orienting response', and it automatically points your eyes and ears in the direction of movement or sound. Crucially, the computational work required to achieve this feat never gets any further than the Superior Colliculus, so by the time you are consciously aware of what you are looking at, your eyes have already been pointing at it for some time. A similar response orients your eyes in the direction of new sounds. Just imagine for a moment the calculations required to achieve that, and remember that all of that takes place in the most basic area of your brain. Your brain takes two images or sounds which arrive at different angles, tracks changing signal levels across a two dimensional surface (your retina), computes a three dimensional location, translates that into a two dimensional muscle movement and then continues to track that changing signal over time as the object in question moves across your visual field.

The shape of your ears causes echoes which perform a task similar to what modern 'Digital Signal Processors' can do. Those echoes cause different frequencies to arrive at your inner ear at different times, with the result that you can detect the three dimensional origin of a sound, even though you only have two ears.

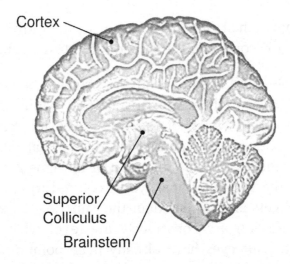

Cortex

Superior Colliculus

Brainstem

In the image above, you can see the folded or 'convoluted' cortex, wrapped around the central areas of the brain. Those layers are pretty much the same, regardless of which part of the cortex we look at, which is very interesting indeed, and certainly fits with what we know of the brain's 'plasticity'; its ability to reorganise itself in case of damage. Nerve tissue apparently never regrows (although it does), but the brain can move functions around in order to bypass areas that have been damaged by injury or perhaps a stroke.

A typically simplified model of perception that you might learn about on a NLP course looks like this:

Reception   Perception   Comprehension

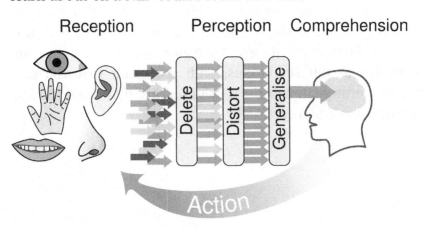

This model implies that perception happens in only one direction, and action also happens only in one direction. If we mapped this simplified model onto the structure of the brain, we might represent the chain of connections as follows:

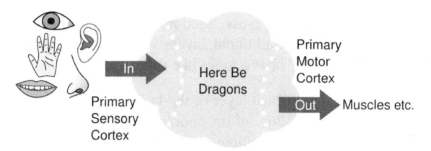

However, our brains are not wired up that way; there are connections running back in the opposite direction too.

The cortex is made up of a number of distinct layers, distinct in that they look different when studied under a microscope. Traditionally, there are six layers, and in some regions of the brain, those six layers are further divided into sub-layers.

Connections can be traced between the layers, and if we take a functional view of the brain rather than a structural one, it would appear that there are in fact four functional layers. A structural view would be to say that because something is built differently, it must be different. A functional view says that because something functions differently, it must be different.

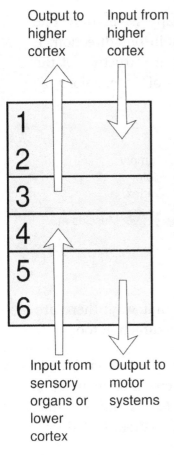

Output to higher cortex

Input from higher cortex

Input from sensory organs or lower cortex

Output to motor systems

A horse and a car are structurally different but functionally similar. A telephone directory and a romantic novel are structurally similar but functionally different.

A cross section, grouping the six traditional layers into four functional layers, looks like this diagram.

Each layer of the brain looks like some kind of transport interchange, not with a simple 'in' and 'out' but with connections both in and out at both the 'top' and the 'bottom'. But what purpose could these extra connections possibly serve?

The answer might be found within the mysterious region of the model where 'thinking' happens, whatever that means. Unlike frogs and earthworms, we do not react to the outside world directly, we react to a simulation of it, and that simulation contains what we could call our 'desired state'. Whilst our eyes may orient themselves automatically towards movement, our 'higher functions' such as being able to identify a moving object, determine if it poses a threat and decide what to do about it are most definitely influenced by factors such as past experiences and current emotional state. A very simplified description of the theory is as follows.

Within our brains, nerve cells hold a copy of what is happening in the outside world, as sampled through our sensory organs. They work like an old fashioned cathode ray tube television screen, holding a complete, apparently moving image which at any given instant really only comprises a single tiny dot of light, moving quickly across the screen in carefully organised and synchronised rows.

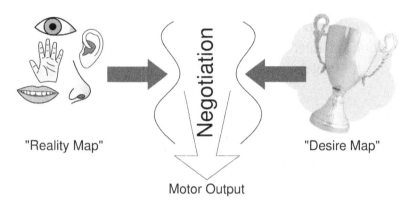

"Reality Map"   "Desire Map"

Motor Output

Other nerve cells hold a copy of what we would like to be happening in the outside world, as defined by our needs and desires. More nerve cells compare the two 'maps' and try to reduce the differences between the two by modifying their outputs to motor systems such as muscles and the endocrine system.

At each layer of processing, the cells and connections in the cortex seek to minimise the difference between the incoming 'present state' signals and the internally connected 'desired state' signals. Just like the thermostat on your central heating, the system takes action to achieve a specific goal, and when that goal has been achieved, the output of the system reduces. This is known as a 'servo system', where the operator sets an output and the system modifies itself to achieve that output. A servo system needs its current state and target state to be reasonably close to each other – too far apart and the system swings out of control because the feedback gap is too great, like setting your air conditioning target temperature and then opening all the windows.[3]

Our brains, like many of the automated systems that you use in your home or office, are 'servo systems', they direct behaviour towards a goal. Imagine a toy car which has a very simply arrangement of a motor, wheels and some kind of sensor to direct it towards a target. The car's guidance system doesn't need to be accurate, it only needs to keep focus on the target. The car's path will look something like this:

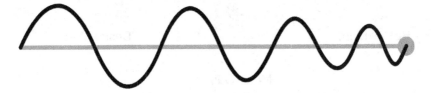

The car is 'off course' for most of its journey, yet it still gets there. That's what your behaviour is like as you direct yourself towards your goals. Sometimes, it will feel like you're moving backwards, but that doesn't matter. What matters is that you are moving.

It's hard to imagine such complexities and subtleties of human behaviour working in such a simple way, until you take into account the fact that, in your brain, there is a nerve 'map' for every nerve ending, every cell on your retina, every taste bud, every muscle and every hair follicle, to name but a few. Those external connections are combined and integrated through these successive layers of processing, until a complex behaviour such as 'drive to the shops' can be de-constructed into a script of muscle

3   This has important implications for personal and organisational change which I explore in my book Change Magic, It turns out we don't have to force people through the Kubler-Ross grief roller-coaster, after all.

The NLP Trainer Training Manual

movements, sensory inputs and rational decisions that begins with hearing an advert on the radio for a delicious new chocolate bar.

I believe that not only is this the most realistic, practical and accurate model of brain function, it also happens to fit very neatly with other models and theories which are equally practical, such as Gallese and Goldman's Simulation Theory and even Eric Berne's Transactional Analysis.

Steve Grand's work is fascinating because he is not a neurologist and he has not arrived at his design for Lucy by trying to understand the mind but instead by trying to replicate the brain. Coincidentally, the test of a model is similar; can you reproduce the results of the person whose talent you have modelled?

Another important aspect of these 'backwards' connections is their ability to modify input. As babies develop their neural wiring, they become accustomed to certain inputs, learning to prioritise the importance of different stimuli. We are extremely economical and efficient machines, so neural connections which are not used are erased. A chemical called Oxytocin allows synaptic connections to 'dissolve' and be replaced with new ones, and it is the chemical of both learning and love. Neuroscientists have even theorised that the production of Oxytocin, which increases when we fall in love, allows us to forgive and forget, or at least to forget, by literally dissolving old memories and patterns of behaviour. If you want to change the habit of a lifetime, fall head over heels in love with someone who discourages it.

Our eyes and ears are receptive to a certain range of stimuli. For example, we can see light in a frequency range which we perceive as running from red through to violet. We see the colours of a rainbow, not because they are 'there' but because our eyes detect frequencies of light in a certain way. We know that some insects can see in what we would call the 'ultraviolet' range, and we know that dogs can hear in what we would call the 'ultrasound' range. Our sensory organs have evolved specifically for the purpose of living on Earth, so it's no surprise that both the retinal cells of our eyes and the chlorophyll in plants are optimised for working in sunlight.

When we start to build more complex structures on top of these basic sensory systems, something interesting happens. Language is a good example, because it is so incredibly complex. Our ability to convert an experience into an abstract set of symbols and then convey those symbols to another person – or even a dog – in such a way that the original experience, or something like it, is recreated in the mind of the receiver is nothing short of miraculous. Our ability to hear language is learned, and our ability to learn is influenced by the production of Oxytocin. If you want to learn a new language, go to classes with someone you love.

While our natural production of Oxytocin declines past childhood, we can restart it by choosing to try out new experiences, keeping our brains active, fit and healthy.

One of the hardest things about learning a new language is hearing the different sounds or phonemes that make up that language. Whilst English and French, for example, have many different words for the same things, the basic sounds of the vowels and consonants are quite similar, and certainly similar enough that you could get through a holiday with a phrase book. But what about English compared to Finnish or Japanese? Some of the phonemes are very different, a stereotypical example being that native

Japanese speakers struggle with the sound of the letter 'R', pronouncing it as a 'L'. As a Japanese baby grows, it hears only Japanese language and so its remarkably economical brain develops only the necessary connections. A native Japanese speaker doesn't only struggle with 'R' because they're not used to saying it, they struggle because their brains are unable to process the sound of 'R', so they never develop the connections required to say it. As a baby, they never hear it, so they never develop the connections to make sense of and replicate it. Even in England, we struggle to pronounce place names in Scotland and Wales, simply because we're not used to the way that 'LL', 'DD' and 'GH' are used, and many of us struggle to understand the 'broadest' regional accents, simply because we're not used to hearing them.

The point here is that these reverse connections modify sensory input in order to simplify processing and cognition. If you were building a computer system to analyse images, such as a car number plate recognition system, you would want to reduce the amount of computational power required as much as possible, because that will optimise the system's response time and accuracy. If you could use a camera which only received light around the yellow range of the visible spectrum, it would emphasise the number plates on the back of British cars and reduce the amount of information for the computer to process.

The sensory capability of our eyes and ears is modified by our experiences so that we become more attuned to seeing and hearing what we expect.

Michael Merzenich is another name worth looking up; he has been working in the field of 'neuroplasticity' for many years and has pioneered a revolution in neurology; a revolution which has shaken the previously accepted model that brain functions are localised into functional areas that cannot be changed once a person leaves their childhood. Merzenich's work shows that the brain reorganises itself surprisingly quickly when recovering from damage or adapting to new experiences. Some of his experiments, and those of others in the field, have involved mapping the individual connections between sensory receptors and the cortex, showing that there is a one to one mapping between the various senses and the processing centres of the brain. For example, there is a topographical map of the skin within the brain, meaning that the map is the same overall shape as the real thing. The area of your brain where your right index finger tip connects to is next to the area where your right thumb tip connects to, however that won't be in precisely the same place as it is in my brain.

You can read more about Merzenich's research in any of his publications or papers, or in 'The Brain that Changes Itself' by Normal Doidge, a popular science book which collects a number of different fields of research to add weight to the argument that the brain never stops growing, changing and learning.

Personally, I find it more surprising that scientists ever believed the brain to be immutable. After all, you are learning from these words as you read them now. Could it really be possible that your brain is acquiring new knowledge *without* changing in some way? Why should learning from a new experience be significantly different to learning a new language or recovering the use of a limb after nerve damage?

Where, you may ask, does this research fit with cognitive or behavioural psychology? The 'desire map' is an obvious analogy for a goal, belief, value, outcome or need. It doesn't really matter which of those words we use, because the end result is the same - an intention to modify the world to meet our expectations. Whether I want an interviewer for a job to be scary, or whether I just know deep down that they will be, even though I don't want that, the result is the same; a scary interviewer. What this gives us is two important things:

1. A way to reveal and perhaps modify those hidden behavioural drivers

2. A way to modify the 'desire map' that directs our behaviour and the results that we achieve

We could say that the brain's purpose is to direct external behaviour so that the difference between present and desired state is minimised, but that then raises the question of where the desired state comes from. Sometimes, regardless of what long term plans we make, our short term behaviour seems to lead us round in the same circles.

Clearly, certain essential biological processes can drive the desire map; thirst or hunger, for example. But where does a desire map for a promotion or for recognition from one's peers come from?

Steve Grand proposed that our brains comprise layers upon layers of such maps which each have their own short term goals and form part of a larger, far more complex pattern of behaviour. Certainly, we could relate a need for food or security to a job promotion through a chain of connected beliefs. One role of coaching or counselling is to challenge those beliefs so that a person may meet their needs more effectively.

The goal of any living organism is homeostasis; an equilibrium that keeps the organism healthy and alive. Life is a delicate balance, for example between staying in the safety of the cave, risking starvation and heading out to forage, risking being eaten by a predator. Your body temperature, blood oxygenation and stomach acid level must all be maintained within carefully controlled ranges, and either too much or too little can be fatal.

While homeostasis is a good thing at a level of basic bodily functions, it's not so useful for humans with career aspirations and other long term goals, because it tends to keep you exactly where you are. Many psychotherapeutic approaches work with 'life scripts'; behaviours learned during our childhood that are no longer appropriate for us yet which repeat as if on autopilot. We know this when we act like our parents and promise to stop, yet we hear the same words coming out of our mouths as if someone else is in the driving seat.

We need to be able to break the connection between past experiences and future expectations, and having done that, we need to create a new desired state which is appropriate for the way that we want our lives to be.

To summarise, the purpose and function of a brain is to minimise the difference between an organism's present and desired states. NLP give us a set of tools for minimising the differences between that perceived present state and 'objective reality', and also for modifying the desired state so that it reflects our conscious, long term plans rather than our unconscious, learned, repetitive behaviours.

4.1.1.1   Modelling the Learning Process

As a NLP Master Practitioner, you should be able to model a behavioural process.

Therefore, you should be able to model the way that someone learns.

First, start with your definition of learning, so that you can focus on the specific behaviours involved.

Think about how you can test your model – could you use it to improve the way that someone learns something?

5 Learning Theories

Our knowledge of learning is based on our research into psychology, and how the mind learns is a fundamental aspect of how the mind works.

There are broadly four views on this, however they are not mutually exclusive. In fact, I think they're all true, and that the overall learning process is a combination.

Behaviourist – learning as behaviour change or conditioning

Cognitivist – learning as understanding

Constructivist – learning as construction of knowledge

Social – learning as social practice

Each of these is a group of theories and models, and you should familiarise yourself with them through further reading.

5.1.1 Behaviourist

Behaviourist learning focuses on 'doing'.

Behaviourists propose that learning is a change in behaviour resulting from an acquired adaptation to an external stimulus. This is 'black box' thinking, in that we don't know what's inside the black box or how it works, we can only know its inputs and outputs. Therefore, its inputs and outputs are the only things which exist.

Pavlov trained his dogs in 1927, and Skinner trained pigeons and people in 1953. What all of these experiments, and more, have in common is that when you present a living organism with a consistent stimulus, it will begin to exhibit a persistent, consistent response.

Behaviourism proposes that people can be conditioned or 'trained' to behave in certain ways if clear objectives are specified. They don't have to think about what they're doing, they don't even have to understand what they're doing, they just have to do it, in response to a stimulus. For example, when a face appears in front of you, say, "Do you want an apple pie with that?"

Behaviourism, at its most limited, assumes that people are like machines, passive, unemotional, and that the trainer has perfect knowledge. A purely behaviourist approach allows no room for individuality, self expression or improvisation. All too often, corporate trainers use a behaviourist approach and then managers complain that their staff don't have any initiative. You simply can't train people to perform mechanistic actions and then complain when they don't think for themselves.

A key aspect of behaviourism as a training approach is reinforcement through reward, so having trained someone to perform a simple task, and having rewarded them for that behaviour, it's now even harder to get them to use their initiative, at which point we need a culture change program to reset the behaviours. Alternatively, you could read my book Change Magic and save yourself all that trouble.

The main problem with a purely behaviourist approach is that people are, of course, not machines, and do ultimately reach the point where their need for self determinism over-rides their need for obedience. Like the Cylons or NS-5s[4] or Replicants or Skynet or Dark Star's nuclear bomb, the working classes will always rise up and overthrow their masters.

---

4   I know, VIKI was behind it all really.

5.1.2 Cognitivist

Cognitivist learning focuses on 'knowing'.

Cognitive learning is the processing, assimilation and adpatation of new pieces of information. In 1971, Jean Piaget conducted famous experiments which are still valuable in our understanding of the development of brain function through childhood.

Assimilation is the simple integration of new facts, whereas accommodation is the adaptation of mental maps to incorporate new information.

New species of dinosaurs are regularly discovered which add to our understanding of life on Earth prior to our modern age. Every now and then, a fossil is found which overturns what we thought we knew. For example, many dinosaurs had early feathers, and in February 2017 the fossilised remains of a pregnant dinosaur was found, showing that not all dinosaurs laid eggs, some gave birth to live young.

Finding new types of dinosaur that fit our existing models of what they looked like is an example of assimilation. Finding a feathered or pregnant dinosaur is an example of adaptation.

Cognitive learning is the process of organising your experiences to integrate new experiences so that you maintain a personal model of how the world works.

Cognitive dissonance is the name that psychologists give to a person's inability to integrate a new experience into their world map, for example, if you met a visitor from another planet or if your teenage child cleaned up after themselves.

It is often easier to reject the new information completely than to change the map in order to accommodate it.

Cognitive learning theories relate to thought processes such as perception, cognition, encoding, memory, and how these are used to acquire, process and retain information. Of course, we now know that these are not distinct processes, so whilst learning certainly has a cognitive component, it cannot be exclusively cognitive.

In a cognitive approach, we help students to understand how they make sense of new knowledge and we give them ways to organise information such as Tony Buzan's 'mind mapping' or Bloom's taxonomy of learning.

Even in NLP Practitioner training, we give students a model of subjective sensory experience upon which they will build their understanding that the world is not the way they think it is, and that in fact the world is exactly the way they think it is. Such paradoxes serve as a framework for new experiences which could otherwise be unsettling and even frightening. For example, in a perceptual positions exercise, a student could form a very different perception of their parents than they have done up to that point, and realise that they always had the power to change that relationship. This uncomfortable realisation can lead to denial or cognitive dissonance which causes them to reject the content of the training as a trick or quick fix. By giving students a theoretical framework, even one which the trainer arbitrarily constructed, the risk of such rejection is minimised.

You can see the biggest problem with cognitive approaches – the trainer is largely in control of the learning content and the theoretical framework used to minimise the chance of rejection. The pressure is therefore on the trainer to keep their knowledge up to date, and as I've already said about the majority of NLP trainers, that simply doesn't happen. Your need for self expression is not because you are right brain dominant.

One of the other drawbacks with a purely cognitive approach is that the demonstration of knowledge is the measure of success, not the application of that knowledge. I know how to make cold calls, how to sell, how to gather customer needs and so on. But work in a call centre? I doubt that I could do it. I know how to do it, but I don't want to do it. I know how to build a wall but give me a pile of bricks and the outcome might be different to what you had in mind.

5.1.3 Constructivist

Cognitivist learning focuses on 'creating'.

The cognitive model proposes that we largely create our reality by integrating new ideas and then projecting those ideas onto the world.

Knowledge is not something 'out there' waiting to be collected, like pebbles on a beach, as Isaac Newton may or may not have said. Instead, we are the creators of our perceptions, the directors of our own life stories. This idea gives us a way of explaining how different people can have very different perceptions of the same events.

In constructivist theories such as those put forward by George Kelly (1955), the student is absolutely central to the learning, and the role of the trainer is to create experiences which lead the learners to form their own understandings and develop their own insights which are then part of each individual's map of the world.

We assume that learners are driven, not by reward or threats, but by their need to find meaning and significance in the world, and we assume that they learn best through active engagement in new experiences, problem solving, analysis, planning and reflection.

5.1.4 Experiential Learning

Experiential learning methods are one example of constructivist learning, the idea being that people learn from reflecting on their own experiences rather than by being spoon-fed information.

Theorists such as John Dewey (1938), Kurt Lewin (1951), David Kolb (1984), Boud *et al* (1993) and Russ Vince (2002) have all developed experiential learning theories, and we'll be exploring Kolb's in much more detail later on.

Experiential learning requires a focus on the individual to create their own learning through action and reflection. The trainer has to design experiences and provide time for reflection, and if the learners are not used to thinking for themselves, the trainer might have to provide some structure for that reflective process, perhaps through a series of questions.

Constructivist learning theories might explain why people differ in the ways they engage with the same learning process and how their learning from the same experiences can vary greatly. Behaviourist and cognitivist theories cannot explain such individual differences. Learning is dependent on much more than the knowledge of the trainer or the content of the training materials. Many corporate trainers simply don't have the luxury of time to explore such individualisation, and the pressure to create conformity forces them down a behaviourist or cognitive route. Other corporate trainers are, of course, just not very good and lack the facilitation skills required to make the most of an experiential process.

Sometimes, we don't want people to create their own learning. If you're training flight crews to operate safety equipment, you don't necessarily want them to create their own ideas and routines. However, they still benefit from creating their own sense of purpose and meaning, even in a simple, repetitive task.

5.1.5 Social Learning

Social learning focuses on 'sharing'.

Our thought processes and our communication systems are intrinsically linked. We talk to ourselves and we signal our internal experiences to others. Social learning theories propose that a person cannot learn in isolation, they must be part of some social network in order to reflect on and share their experiences. People make sense of new ideas and are able to create a sense of meaning only through dialogue and interaction with others, an idea that is called social constructivism.

The idea that social interaction is important in learning was created by Levs Vygotsky (1978), who observed that children were able to perform well above expectations for their age if given the chance to interact with someone older. He is known for the concept 'zone of proximal development', the idea that we learn best at the edge of familiarity – not too stretched and not too comfortable, and that social interaction helps to create the right level of challenge more effectively than an individual can alone. It seems obvious really – we cannot see our own limits, so it's only through social interaction that we can see what others are capable of and therefore what is possible. If you play a sport, you're unlikely to learn much by playing people who are less skilled than you. To get better, you have to get beaten. A lot.

Jerome Bruner (1996) and Etienne Wenger (1998) both researched the impact of social culture on learning, and if we define a culture simply as a system of rules then we shouldn't be surprised that those rules will affect learning.

Social constructivism adds the idea that team working, collaboration and competition are valuable aspects of the learning environment.

The role of the trainer changes from the provider of knowledge to the custodian of the environment. Equality and mutual respect are vital within the learning group, and once we put a group of people together we start to see signs of social bias which the trainer has to work to overcome.

Overall, though, if you're going to train people in groups then you're going to see evidence of social learning, and developing your facilitation skills is vital if you're to manage this effectively.

5.2 Hybrid Learning

I said earlier that I don't believe that these different styles and theories are isolated from each other, and we can't think in terms of which one is right and which is wrong. All are descriptions of what a theorist can observe, and from our NLP point of view, that means that they can be modelled. However, what I believes colours those observations for anyone not versed in NLP is fear. Learning represents change, and change can be scary, and barriers to learning will shape the way that a person learns.

For example, Honey and Mumford took Kolb's learning cycle and turned it into four learning styles. Even though these categories, known as 'types' have long been discredited for all psychometric or pseudo-psychometric tools, trainers still describe their learners as 'activists' or 'reflectors'. Mind you, NLP trainers still describe their students as 'visual' or 'auditory', which is just as bad.

An activist is someone who jumps straight in and starts experimenting. A reflector is someone who stands back and observes others. From a NLP process point of view, if both learners can provide some commentary on their experience then they are both engaged in the process of experiencing; one first hand, one second hand. What I'm suggesting is that the second person is not a reflector, they are an activist who is afraid to have a go – afraid in case they make a mistake, or get it wrong, or get into trouble, or break something, or worst of all, make a fool of themselves. Doing something new means that your confidence will be lower than usual. The last thing you need is to hear your colleagues laughing at your pathetic attempts to build a tower out of matchsticks or operate a fire extinguisher. So, if you have learned during your early life that mistakes are a source of ridicule then it's easier to play safe and let others go first. I can't prove this hypothesis, I can only comment on the hundreds of learners who I've worked with. I also think that we can learn a lot from watching children. At your local park or play centre, you can see the children with pushy parents who are reluctant to try something new. The parents project their own fear of failure and their children learn that it's bad to get something wrong. They have no idea why, they just know that it's bad. This is itself an example of behavioural learning, where the child learns a response without the rationale for that response – the cognitive part. The child learns to react a certain way without the choice of when to act that way. There are times that we can all benefit from standing back and letting some other idiot go first, but what we must all have is that choice over our actions. Without cognitive understanding and choice, we are automatons, programmed to perform tasks with no understanding of why or when to perform those tasks. Our evolved brains allow us to process a stimulus and, instead of automatically reacting to it, making a choice about how to respond. The greater the autonomy of learning, the greater the autonomy of behaviour.

We learn simple repetitive actions, useful for handshakes and opening doors. We learn facts, useful when shouting at the TV during quiz shows. We create knowledge, useful when we are generalising our experience of life and making career choices. We learn with others, useful in adapting to new relationships and in surviving corporate team building events. We learn all of this, not in discrete chunks but in one continuous process of experiencing, reflecting, generalising and projecting. Our lives are both the giver of our life's knowledge and the product of it.

The NLP Trainer Training Manual

The Learning
Cycle

Like day and night, like the passage of the seasons, learning is a cycle.

In 1984, David Kolb and Ron Fry published Kolb's Experiential Learning Model (ELM). Kolb's work is greatly respected across many learning fields, from schools to professional education. The ELM presents a four part learning cycle.

6.1.1 Concrete Experience - Feel

This stage is one of real, physical, direct, first hand, visceral sensory experience. An experience might comprise any combination of sights, sounds, feelings, tastes or smells and in fact, you may know that all experiences and therefore all memories comprise all of these elements, even though some of them may be less prominent than others. A concrete experience is external to us and therefore always in the present.

6.1.2 Reflective Observation - Watch

Once we've had a concrete experience, we reflect on it. We cast our mind back, both consciously and unconsciously, and relive the experience so that we can make generalisations and draw conclusions. Research has shown that the structure within the brain known as the hippocampus creates a kind of 'action replay' of emotionally charged events, etching them forever in our long term memories. Reflective observation is internal to us and therefore always in the past, and the observation isn't necessarily visual, it features all of the sensory information which was originally present.

6.1.3 Abstract Concept - Think

Having relived the experience, we take those generalisations and conclusions and use them to create an abstract concept, a set of rules or principles which govern the experience and others like it. When abstract conceptualisation involves mental rehearsal, it is internal and appears to be in the future, when in fact it is a replay of the past as the future doesn't yet exist.

6.1.4 Active Experiment - Do

We take the abstract concept and test it by applying it to new situations. A child tests a range of household objects to find out if they float as well as his lost balloon. A father gives all of the house plants a close shave in order to 'try out' the new hedge trimmer that he received for his birthday. Active experimentation leads full circle to a new concrete experience which either affirms or contradicts the abstract concept. Active experimentation is always external and in the present.

6.1.4.1   Learning Cycle Examples

What examples can you think of that demonstrate the learning cycle?

Can you think of any counter-examples?

Try learning something by deliberately missing stages of the cycle.

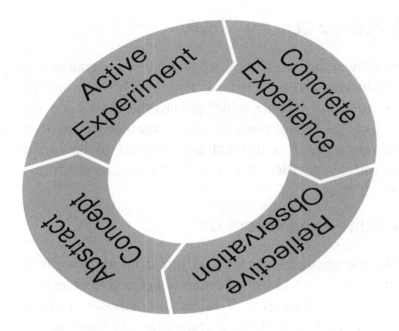

We could perhaps say that the sequence of events is:

1. Do something

2. Get feedback

3. Review feedback

4. Make a plan

You may not be consciously aware of this process, yet if you think about it, you can notice how every experience you have results from some action, and every conscious action results from some kind of mental rehearsal. When you take action, the very first thing that happens is that you see and hear the result of your actions. Put this all together and you live a cycle of reception and projection, where past events are projected onto future expectations.

6.2 Honey & Mumford Learning Styles

Onto Kolb's four learning stages, Peter Honey and Alan Mumford later mapped the four roles shown in the diagram below; Activist, Pragmatist, Theorist and Reflector.

6.2.1 Activist

Activists need to do something and they learn by experimenting. They need to experience something for themselves and work out how they feel about it, so they make decisions based on their instincts more than on logic. Activists seek hands on experience.

Activists say, "Can I have a go?"

6.2.2 Pragmatist

Pragmatists like to do what works. They like to know what works in the real world. Pragmatists like to find practical applications for ideas.

Pragmatists say, "Does it work?"

6.2.3 Theorist

Theorists like to observe what's going on and then form a theory or opinion about it. Theorists like evidence, logical explanations, abstract models, facts and figures. They don't like subjectivity.

Theorists say, "How does it work?"

6.2.4 Reflector

Reflectors like to observe and reflect and turn things around from different points of view. They like to use their imagination to solve problems rather than diving in like the activists. They like to take time to ponder and don't rush into decisions until they think that they have covered all the angles.

Reflectors say, "Let me think about it."

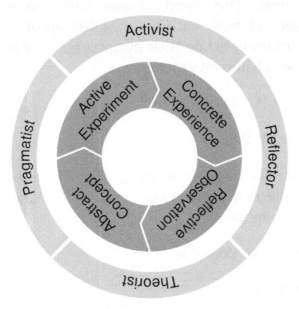

The huge, huge problem with learning styles is that they are not true. In fact, all type indicators are problematic, because someone decided that there are a certain number of fixed types of people, and you then have to shoe-horn everyone into those fixed types. People are far simpler, and far more complex at the same time.

A person isn't one kind of learner, they are all four, in the sequence that is constrained by the laws of physics. You cannot get feedback from an action until you have performed that action. As far as physicists are currently aware, time only flows in one direction – a concept recently strengthened by the discovery that some atoms are not spherical but are pear shaped, giving the universe a unidirectional imbalance.

People are not fixed in these roles, they are preferences. We all need time to reflect, we all need to take part, we all need to create rules and we all need personal experience to confirm those rules.

A complete learning experience must always involve the full cycle because that reflects how our life experiences are formed. Life happens, we ponder on it, we wonder what it all means and then figure out what to do about it. We probably don't have a great deal of control over life as a learning experience which happens whether we like it or not, but Kolb's work gives us a language and a framework for understanding what happens when a person *intentionally sets out to learn something new*.

This probably calls to mind the idea of 'conscious incompetence'. When I know that I don't know something, I set out to learn it. I know that I want to record my favourite TV show, but I can't for the life of me remember how to program the video recorder.[5]

However, when learning is not motivated by the individual, the idea of 'unconscious incompetence' is more relevant. I have no idea that there are such things as superconductors, or cytoblasts, or actuaries, and that's generally because I had no interest in them. Should I become interested, just because someone else thinks that it's important for me to know about such things?

---

5 Younger readers may not know what a video recorder is. Google it.

There is no doubt that, during training courses, I have observed learners who like to get stuck in and have a go, learners who prefer to stand back and watch, learners who like to question the theory and learners who like to challenge the utility of what they are learning. However, I put it to you that these are not demonstrations of learning styles, they are demonstrations of how easily people will distract from their own fear of failure, or fear of looking stupid.

Activist	"I'll have a go and see what happens"
Pragmatist	"Prove to me that I won't look stupid by telling me that this works for other people"
Theorist	"Prove to me that I won't look stupid by telling me the theory as to why this works"
Reflector	"I feel stupid. I'll just watch"

A learner has no capacity to understand the theory or case studies behind a topic that they're learning because, by definition, they don't know about the topic. Therefore, their questions are a challenge to the trainer and they will judge the response based not on the factual content of the trainer's reply but on the trainer's congruence during their reply. And since congruence is simply a harmony of verbal and non verbal communication channels, if the trainer wholeheartedly believes the nonsense they're spouting, it will be good enough for the Pragmatists and Theorists.

The Pragmatists and Theorists openly challenge the trainer and are therefore probably Extroverts, whereas the Activist and Reflector just do their own thing and are probably Introverts.

Extroversion and Introversion are nothing to do with how lively someone is, it's about their reference point for sensory comparisons. Extroverts check externally, introverts check internally. Neither is better, we need both, or at least society has been shaped by both and consequently needs both.

Studies of brain plasticity show that a realistic time to master a new behaviour is about six months, with daily practice, reflection and integration. It's interesting that the most current work in neuroscience seems to confirm what teachers have said for generations; that students need regular practice over a prolonged period of time with proper rest in order to truly master a new skill. A good night's sleep really is part of the learning process.

6.3 Other Learning Styles

There are many other 'learning styles' models, such as NLP's sensory model or Gardner's 'Multiple Intelligences'. None of these models are true or false, they're just a way of organising how we think about learning so that we have a language to talk about how we can do it better.

While everyone is an individual, with their own learning style, preference and process, everyone is also subject to the laws of physics, and ye cannae change the laws of physics, Jim[6]

The more conformity that you have in your delivery, the less likely it is that all learners will be able to fully engage.

---

6 According to Star Trek's Chief Engineer, Montgomery 'Scotty' Scott, who has probably the least imaginative nickname in history.

However, fully engaging all learners according to their individual styles can be very time consuming for the trainer, so there has to be a 'happy medium'.

Many trainers talk about a NLP view of learning styles, assigning the labels of Visual, Auditory and Kinaesthetic to learners. I've heard people say, "I'm a visual learner so I need to see a diagram". Duh. We're all visual learners. And what's a kinaesthetic learner? They have to rub themselves up against the powerpoint slides? Oh, they learn by doing. And how do they know what they're doing ? Ah, they see and hear it. And we have the problem that what we call 'kinaesthetic' is an amalgam of quite a few other senses, of which there at least 21 in total, maybe more, not 5.

This 'NLP learning styles' model came from metaprograms which, frankly, I don't believe in. As far as we know, there is no construct within the human brain or mind to create these arbitrary distinctions. At best, there is one, the intraversion/extraversion switch which is thrown within days of birth, based on our parents' level of responsiveness to our needs. I believe that all of the other projections that we call metaprograms can be extrapolated from that reference bias in different contexts, and even that is a stretch, and the whole thing might be an illusion based only on where you are focusing at any given moment.

According to The Guardian[7], "Learning styles are often referred to as VAK – students are categorised as visual, auditory or kinaesthetic learners. This myth states that students will learn more if they are taught in a way that matches their preferred style. Despite an absence of any

---

7   www.theguardian.com/teacher-network/2016/feb/24/four-
    neuromyths-still-prevalent-in-schools-debunked

evidence to support this claim, research carried out in 2012 found it was believed by 93% of teachers in the UK."

Not surprisingly, using multiple senses and activities is far more effective than trying to appeal to any individual, fictitious learning style. The irony is that a teacher, trying to appeal to a classroom of different learning styles actually responds by trying to cover all styles at the same time, which is probably a good idea. Learning styles as individual categories don't exist, however it is true that we acquire information in multiple ways, so if a teacher can cover those multiple ways, they stand a better chance of increasing learning retention than if they stand at the front of the room reading from a book.

Here's an extract from the conclusion of some recent research[8] on the subject, carried out at Cambridge University in the UK.

"An interesting analogy is provided by Clark, who was discussing language, but whose analogy also works for the entire cognitive system. Clark's argument is that we can conceptualise the brain as a 'loose-knit, distributed representational economy' (Clark, 2006[9]). Some elements in the economy might conflict with other elements in the economy, but this is inevitable, as there is no 'homunculus' or single central overseer who determines learning. Rather, there are many interacting parts of the overall reasoning machinery that the brain is maintaining at the same time. The activity of all of these parts is what the child brings to the classroom, and different parts are more or less affected

---

8 www.cne.psychol.cam.ac.uk/pdfs/publication-
   pdfs/Goswami_JOPE_42_3-4_381-399_2008.pdf
9 Clark, A. (2006) Language, Embodiment, and the Cognitive Niche,
   Trends in Cognitive Sciences, 10.8, pp. 370–374.

by different cognitive or emotional experiences. The child brings a 'vast parallel coalition of more-or-less influential forces whose unfolding makes each of us the thinking beings that we are' (ibid.). To borrow from another insightful commentator on the potential of cognitive neuroscience for cognitive development (Diamond, 2007[10]), the truly ambitious goal for education is to cross and integrate the disciplinary boundaries of biology, culture, cognition, emotion, perception and action. Biological, sensory and neurological influences on learning must become equal partners with social, emotional and cultural influences if we are to have a truly effective discipline of education."

In summary, think about learning as an ongoing cyclic process, driven only by the constant stream of data coming in through your senses. There are no styles or fixed preferences, only snapshots in time. We can receive all of the information that our senses have evolved to receive, some of it is useful for supporting future decisions, most of it is useless or irrelevant, and we must have a method for filtering, sorting and archiving that information for later access. That method is the learning cycle.

Plan your training design and delivery to exploit that cycle, because it's happening anyway, whether you like it or not.

10 Diamond, A. (2007) Interrelated and Interdependent, Developmental Science, 10.1, pp. 152–158.

6.4 Reflective Learning

There is a very simple principle underpinning Kolb's observations; that you cannot learn to do something before you have done it. No matter how many times you read the instruction manual, until you perform the act, you cannot complete the feedback loops necessary to fine tune your behaviour.

In The NLP Master Practitioner Manual, I show you how the physical structure of the brain mirrors the process of learning a new task. As a servo control system, the brain, body and sensory systems form part of a feedback loop. The brain creates action in pursuit of a goal, the body implements that action and the senses relate feedback concerning that action.

The complex process that we call 'learning' has nothing to do with reading text books or sitting in classes. It's happening constantly as the brain reinforces the feedback loops which achieve results. The servo system will strengthen the behaviours which achieve their goals. People stay in abusive relationships and take manipulative routes to achieve their goals because, simply, their behaviours 'work'. Is there a 'better' way? Yes and no. Yes because there are alternatives, no because the current 'way' is exactly the way that it is meant to be. You could put paprika into lasagne, but it might not be lasagne any more. Would it be better or worse? Who knows. Try it and see if you like it.

We can only be consciously aware of what we have learned by comparing our experiences over time, looking back. When that comparison creates a preference, we call that 'learning'. Through this wonderful process, I discovered a long time ago that a tuna and egg curry is not a recipe to be repeated. But paprika in lasagne? Hmm. I might try it.

Taking action and sensing the results of that action connect the servo system to the outside world.

Reflecting on the experience and planning the next action are more inwardly focused stages of the cycle.

Therefore, a learner's focus of attention must flip between the 'inside' and the 'outside' as their brain generates action, gathers feedback, compares that feedback to the original intention and continues to refine that action.

Our brains simply aren't built to learn by listening to long transmissions of words or by reading academic text books. Everyone is an active learner.

Now, consider how this applies to your training design.

As a trainer, you will have an intention, an outcome. You will take action through your training delivery, Finally, you will gather feedback to determine your success in achieving your outcomes. And at every stage of the training process, you will have loops within loops of outcome, action and feedback at both the conscious and unconscious levels, as in loops which your students will be aware of, and loops which they won't be aware of.

6.5 The Ongoing Learning Cycle

We know that, whatever you do, your learners will learn by moving through the learning cycle. We know that they will copy you, and if that's all that they do, they'll only learn behaviours without the information to know when to use those behaviours. If, as well as slavishly copying you, they learn the theories and reasons behind those behaviours, they'll have a little more flexibility and be able to improvise in order to increase the effectiveness of their behaviours.

If they are then able to try out variations of their own and figure out their own rules, theories and reasons, their improvisations will become even more effective.

Therefore, I think we can all agree that there is some merit in the idea of a learning cycle, and if we put that learning into a social context then individuals will start to share their improvisations with each other, and the knowledge of the individuals will then grow to the level of the group.

All good so far! How, then, do we incorporate this into our training design?

Let's start an imaginary NLP Practitioner training in the way that many trainers do, by talking about the subjective nature of experience. We need to give our learners an experience, and that experience should have them playing an active part, not just sitting there while you prattle on about how amazing the world is. Let's devise a simple activity to give our learners some insight into the subjective nature of their senses by getting them to look at some optical illusions. If we follow Kolb's learning cycle, they would look at the illusions, then think about how those illusions work, then test those illusions with some kind of experiment. It may not be practical for them to design their own illusions, as this is a huge branch of perceptual psychology in itself. Maybe we could do something more practical, such as... what? What do we get our learners to do?

To answer that, we must go back to the reason that we showed them the illusions in the first place. We want to give our learners a personal experience of the subjectivity of their perceptions, which is really not possible because they are using their subjective perceptions to look at their subjective perceptions! Imagine trying to clean a dirty mark off your TV screen without realising it's actually part of the movie you're watching. So by using optical illusions to create a sense of confusion, we demonstrate that the learner's eyes are not creating a reliable, objective sense of external reality, which in turn allows us to introduce the concept of subjective reality that NLP is based on. After all, if our experiences are what they are and we can't change that, then learning NLP is a waste of time.

Some of the common optical illusions you'll see are based on the way that your brain's visual cortex infers qualities such as size and distance from other information such as contrast. I would suggest that, unless you have some psychology researchers in your group, you'll struggle to come up with new illusions, so let's stick to one which is easy to replicate and test – the blind spot. You'll find this one in the start of The NLP Practitioner Manual, and your learners can create their own variations to test the theory.

Concrete Experience	Look at optical illusions
Reflective Observation	Think about how they work
Abstract Concept	Form a theory e.g. blind spot
Active Experiment	Create other blind spot tests

What's next? Let's build on this knowledge of subjective reality by giving our learners a language to talk about their experiences, also known as submodalities.

Concrete Experience	Notice how our experience of events differs
Reflective Observation	Notice any consistencies between those experiences
Abstract Concept	Theorise about experiences which might fit the same pattern
Active Experiment	Find other experiences which fit the pattern

Our innate desire to test our theories gives rise to the phenomenon of confirmation bias, in which we only look for evidence that confirms our beliefs. Get your learners to also look for counter examples, to try to disprove their theories.

For example, in the context of submodalities, if your learners believe they've found a pattern of sad memories being visually dark, get them to look for counter-examples by finding happy memories which are also dark. If they find any, can they explain the discrepancy within their original theory?

So far, so good. We have the first two steps of a NLP Practitioner training, and two practical exercises for your learners. After studying submodalities, you might move on to a technique which exploits submodalities, such as anchoring or swish. And here we have a problem. Let's say that this is your course design so far:

Subjectivity	Submodalities	Anchoring	Swish

Within each step, you have a learning cycle, which is super. But what you have also inadvertently created is a series of isolated chunks of content with no connection between them, other than you saying, "And now we'll move on to..."

As a corporate trainer delivering training on time management or basic communication skills, this is to be expected. As a NLP trainer, you have to work a bit harder. Partly, this is because your training programs are not one day events, they span multiple days and perhaps even multiple modules over many weeks or months. Once your learners have gone home for the night, they will forget a lot of what they have experienced. The next morning, if you start with your next chunk of content, you'll find that your learners will struggle more than if you had only covered it a few minutes previously.

In NLP, and in most training in fact, information is not contained in neat, isolated segments, it is all woven together to form a complete entity. However, because of the linear nature of time, we can't train the whole thing at once, so we have no realistic choice but to train in logical chunks.

6.5.1 Forgetting

Rather than rewrite the theory, I'll quote from good old Wikipedia.

"In 1885, Hermann Ebbinghaus extrapolated the hypothesis of the exponential nature of forgetting. The following formula can roughly describe it:

$$R = e^{(t/s)}$$

where R is memory retention, S is the relative strength of memory, and t is time.

The Forgetting Curve

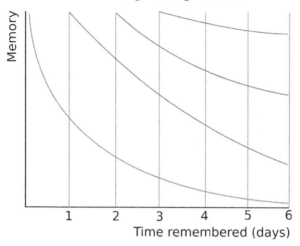

Time remembered (days)

Hermann Ebbinghaus ran a limited, incomplete study on himself and published his hypothesis in 1885 as Über das Gedächtnis (later translated into English as Memory: A Contribution to Experimental Psychology). Ebbinghaus studied the memorisation of nonsense syllables, such as "WID" and "ZOF" by repeatedly testing himself after various time periods and recording the results. He plotted these results on a graph creating what is now known as the "forgetting curve". From his discovery regarding the "forgetting curve", Ebbinghaus came up with the effects of "overlearning". Essentially, if you practiced something more than what is usually necessary to memorize it, you would have effectively achieved overlearning. Overlearning ensures that information is more impervious to being lost or forgotten, and the forgetting curve for this overlearned material is shallower.

Ebbinghaus hypothesized that the speed of forgetting depends on a number of factors such as the difficulty of the learned material (e.g. how meaningful it is), its representation and physiological factors such as stress and sleep. He further hypothesized that the basal forgetting rate differs little between individuals. He concluded that the difference in performance (e.g. at school) can be explained by mnemonic representation skills.

He went on to hypothesize that basic training in mnemonic techniques can help overcome those differences in part. He asserted that the best methods for increasing the strength of memory are:

Better memory representation (e.g. with mnemonic techniques)

Repetition based on active recall (esp. spaced repetition)

His premise was that each repetition in learning increases the optimum interval before the next repetition is needed (for near-perfect retention, initial repetitions may need to be made within days, but later they can be made after years). Later research suggested that, other than the two factors Ebbinghaus proposed, higher original learning would also produce slower forgetting.

Spending time each day to remember information, such as that for exams, will greatly decrease the effects of the forgetting curve. Reviewing material in the first 24 hours after learning information is the optimum time to re-read notes and reduce the amount of knowledge forgotten."

More recently, neuroscientists researched the spaced learning effect[11] by examining reflexes in sea slugs, crayfish and cats, and also by stimulating the neurons in thin slices of rat brain. They discovered that repeated stimuli, at precisely timed intervals, are one of the most reliable ways to commit information to long term memory.

---

11 www.ncbi.nlm.nih.gov/pmc/articles/PMC3782739/ (2013)

So, to summarise, your recall of what you have learned decays exponentially over time, and you can increase your retention through better presentation of learning materials and repetition of active learning experiences. In other words, make it easy for yourself and practice. Remember, though, that practice does not make perfect. Practice makes permanent. You have to practice the right things.

If you have allowed your students time for breaks and sleep then they will forget what you've told them, but if you make them listen to you for 60 hours straight, they'll fall asleep anyway. You just can't win. Unless you happen to like serialised TV dramas.

One of my favourite TV shows used to begin each week with "Previously on Battlestar Galactica". Then, during the opening credits, it would show brief glimpses of what was about to happen. At the end of the show, more brief glimpses would appear to tease viewers with next week's events.

The format of the show itself would open up a number of story 'threads' and then tie these off towards the end of the show. Overall, the design was something like this:

Previously...	Coming up...	Here it is	What's next

As an avid viewer, I never needed to be reminded of what had happened last week because that was the reason I was watching this week. However, TV executives do not rely on viewers being avid fans, they rely on viewers being overwhelmed with other viewing choices, so they use their knowledge of psychology to make life easier for us. Any viewer could 'tune in' at any point in the series and make sense of what was going on.

How could you use this idea in your training design?

If you're a good trainer with typically varied learners then not everything will make sense to everyone in the same way. Sometimes, your learners will 'get it' because of what you say, sometimes because of what they experience, sometimes because of what other learners say, sometimes after they've been away and thought about it, and sometimes they'll just never get it.

"Plan to space out learning so that content is revisited in some engaging way, especially with some sleep in between study sessions, and seek to have people return to the material once on the order of days, once on the order of weeks, and once on the order of months, if possible."

6.5.2 Mix It Up

According to researchers[12], we can only pay attention for around 20 minutes at a time before the neurons that take in new information become 'tired'. That doesn't mean that you have to take a break every 20 minutes, it just means that you can switch to a different format, for example from talking to questioning or from a discussion to an activity, or using videos to break up your training content.

Some NLP trainers argue that they're 'teaching at the unconscious level' and that 'the mind is a learning machine', neither of which is an excuse for a lazy trainer, sitting on a stool at the front of the room, telling tedious stories about how great he or she is. We are trainers, not entertainers.

---

12 www.td.org/Publications/Magazines/TD/TD-
 Archive/2014/01/Keep-An-Eye-on-the-Time (2014)

People are spending their hard earned money with us so that they will acquire tangible, valuable skills. We are not running personal enhancement seminars where our students feel great after the event but never actually make any changes in their lives. There are 'trainers' who use that business model of course, but if you're one of them then you've probably already worked out that this book isn't for you because real NLP Trainer Training is just too much hard work. However, if you value hard work and you want to deliver something to your students which will really make a difference in their lives then you're in the right place.

Decades of thorough, peer-reviewed, scientific research into psychology and neuroscience have given us great insights into what makes learning most effective. Here's a summary, including some tips for you.

State

Make sure your learners are comfortable and that they have had enough sleep and enough to eat and drink. Think in terms of physical, emotional and mental state.

Most NLP trainers will think of anchoring here, I encourage you to forget anchoring because anchoring is not a technique for accessing resource states, anchoring is a means of controlling the delivery of a technique by managing the client's responses. Put anchoring out of your mind for your training delivery. Focus on getting the environment right, with the rule of thumb that if you're comfortable then your learners will be comfortable. A room with no natural light is unlikely to leave you feeling refreshed after a Six Step Reframe.

Relevance

We learn what we need to learn, when we need to learn it. Focus on the reasons that your students came to your training, and give them time to apply what they're learning to their own lives and interests.

The information that you share and the questions that you get your learners to answer prior to the start of your training will get them to focus on the relevance to them, and will influence their state too.

Most of the time, your learners will have self-selected, so they chose to come on the course and they know how it's relevant to them. In corporate training it's more often the case that people are told to go on a training course, whether they think it's relevant or not.

Presentation

Use a variety of presentation methods and resources to convey the same information in different ways. See chapter 10 for some ideas about this, remembering that there are no learning styles and that all of your learners have the capacity to take in information through multiple channels.

Activity

Have as many learning activities as possible; practice sessions, activities, games, experiments, group exercises.

If learners don't have an active role to play in the process, they cannot complete a learning cycle and will disengage.

You'll recall the research which suggests a limit of about 20 minutes on one learning method, so think of it this way: The learning cycle has a 20 minute buffer on the stages where the learner isn't actively using their knowledge. Active experiment enables your learners to test the new information so that they can individualise it and store it for long term access.

Play

Play in learning doesn't mean using toys and games and frivolous junk, as was the case in the 'Brain Friendly Learning' fad. It means active experimentation without fear of judgement or failure.

I feel that there are two main ways that you will create a sense of play in your training; firstly, by being playful yourself and secondly, by framing practice activities as having no expected outcome, with experimentation and learning as the only success criteria.

I've seen some long-established NLP trainers get very upset when a technique didn't work. That's a really great example to set for the learners, don't you think? As you'll see later in the book, I advocate an approach whereby you focus on demonstrating the techniques, not on coaching or therapy with your volunteer. Whether the technique gets an impressive result or not is irrelevant, what you're focusing on is showing your learners how to use it themselves. The less impressive your apparent outcome, the more realistic your learners' expectations will be.

A sense of play encourages active experimentation which is a vital part of the learning cycle.

Variation

Change your training method every 20 minutes or so. This can simply mean that you stop talking and ask a few questions for your learners to think about, or give them a few minutes for a group discussion, or show a video.

Gapping

Take advantage of breaks and modular course formats to repeat learning.

Also consider giving your learners 'homework', even if it's just something to notice on the way home, or a question to think about for the next morning. This bridges together the sections of your training and encourages your learners to think about applications.

If you're running a modular course with weeks or even months between modules then homework is very important. You might email reminders, or additional questions to your learners to keep them focused on the fact that they're still learning, even though they're not in your classroom.

You might also take advantage of the role that dreaming plays in long term memory. Dreaming is a way for our brains to reorganise recent experiences, so you may find that your learners have interesting dreams during the training which you can discuss. At the very least, you can comment that any interesting dreams will be connected.

Repetition

Repeat content in different ways, using presentation, Q&A, discussion, activities etc. to get learners to repeat learning from different angles.

Also link subjects together, for example in techniques where anchoring plays a significant part such as Perceptual Positions, remind your learners that it's a good opportunity to practice their anchoring skills. You then get repetition of important information and skills without having to overtly repeat yourself.

Application

Increase relevance and encourage improvisation by getting learners to apply what they're learning to practical situations.

You might do this through group discussions and case studies, by getting your learners to put together presentations and most importantly by encouraging them to try out their new skills on friends and colleagues and then report back on what they experienced.

Remember: State, Relevance, Presentation, Activity, Play, Variation, Gapping, Repetition, Application.

⁷ Making Plans

Have you ever been to the shops to get one thing, ended up buying lots of things that you liked the look of and then came out without the one thing that you went in for?

A friend of mine asked me to help him with slides for a training workshop. I trimmed his powerpoint file down from 90 slides to about 30 – still too many, but that's the best I could do. He then added back in the ones he couldn't live without and ended up with around 80.

At the end of the day, he called me, excited to tell me how well the day had gone.

"Guess how many slides I got through?" he asked, breathless with exhilaration.

"One", I said.

"Ermmm. Yes, one. How did you know?" he asked, a little deflated.

"Because I know you."

Why did you get home with everything but the one thing you went shopping for? Because you didn't have a shopping list. And you probably also had too much time on your hands.

Why did my friend get through only one slide out of 80? Because he didn't have a learning plan.

And there's no point making a plan if you're not going to stick to it.

I'll be honest, when I first started training NLP, I was more excited about it than my learners were. I experimented and tried different ideas, different techniques. My training courses were different each time. So what? Different students. I'm developing, I'm learning, I'm improving what I do, and each set of students gets the new improved version. That's what I told myself, anyway. In reality, I was playing, experimenting, doing what kept me interested rather than what my students had paid for. Their feedback was that they enjoyed it immensely, but as I did more and more corporate training with large groups, I began to realise that they weren't there to watch me play, they were there to get what they came for. They had a shopping list, I didn't.

Today, my training is fairly consistent, allowing for the specific details of each student's experience. You could come along to day six of any of my Practitioner courses and have the same experience. Does that make my training dull and predictable? Oh, it's never dull! But predictable, yes, which is a very important thing, because it's what your students are paying for.

In the British TV comedy sketch show 'The Fast Show', a husband repeatedly returns from shopping with anything but what his wife sent him out for.

"Hello, dear! How's it going?

Oh, I think I'm on top of it.

Now, did you get the eggs, the butter and the potatoes?

Even better than that! I got some biscuits shaped like radios, a map of Cairo and an ice pick!"

Now, this doesn't mean that you should have a script and say exactly the same words each time. Even if you go to see a live show at a theatre, there will be subtle differences from one performance to the next, because the actors are human, and they are interacting with each other to create a unique, dynamic experience.

In your training, the players, the actors will be different each time, and you'll create an experience which is unique yet which follows the same structure each time.

20 years ago, I told myself that constant reinvention allowed me to improve. It's not true. Reinvention followed by rigorous testing, measurement and comparisons is what allows you to improve. If you don't deliver consistently, you have no benchmark with which to compare yourself. What criteria are you using to measure your performance anyway?

My friend who I mentioned earlier likes to entertain his students. He calls his training 'entertrainment'. If that's what they paid for, that's great. But what's his criteria for measuring his own performance?

More to the point, what's yours?

Having a training plan means that you will stay on track through your training, which in turn means something very important – every activity, and the overall training program, will run on time. I'm sure you've seen trainers or presenters who run out of time and either rush to fit everything in or skip over what they can't cover. It looks unprofessional, and it's very unsatisfying for the audience.

With a plan, you know exactly what you want to cover in your training and you know exactly how long each section should take. My advice is to practice your training and time yourself against your expectations. As a rule of thumb, I usually allow about double the amount of time that I think I need, in other words if I have to fill an hour, I'll prepare for half an hour, 40 minutes at most. The reason for this is very simple. While your learners are engaged in activities, you can watch them and also keep an eye on the time. As long as the time you've allowed is realistic, you can always end the activity on time. However, once you start talking, the hands on your watch will start spinning faster and faster. Even if you write yourself a script, I guarantee that it will take longer once you're performing 'for real'.

The first presentation that I ever delivered at a conference was to 200 customers and I wanted to make sure that I got it 'right'. I wrote myself a script that was exactly 20 minutes long as required, and in fact when I delivered the presentation, the timing was perfect. However, I couldn't read to my timescale and also engage with the audience, and I'm sure that the result was not the most interesting presentation that they had ever seen. Assuming that you want to have some engagement and even fun with your audience, you have to allow additional time. Your script might not explain something as well as you had hoped, and you might have to say more, based on the blank expressions of your learners. You might get questions that you hadn't anticipated. You might remember an amusing story and get sidetracked.

When you have planned your training session to take the full time available, you will run out of time and one of two things will happen; either you will rush to make up time, in which case you aren't doing what you planned, or you will run over time, in which case you have to cut time somewhere else, in which case you aren't doing what you planned. Either way, your plan goes out of the window, and since I presume you made your plan for a very good reason, you are not going to achieve your outcomes.

When I first started running Practitioner training I used to co-train with another trainer. We always got drawn into discussions about applications or ethics, and on the last day of the training we'd run out of time, ironically for the timeline techniques.

These days, my Practitioner and Master Practitioner training runs perfectly to time, every day. Partly it's because I now know how long each technique will take to demonstrate and practice, but mainly it's because I control the conversations that take place between activities.

I can't stress enough how important your timekeeping is. Think about it this way – your students have absolutely no idea whether what you're telling them is technically correct or not, because it's new to them. They have no idea whether the techniques will work in the 'real world', they only have your word for that. The primary evidence upon which they will base their trust in you is whether you seem to know what you're doing. If your timekeeping is out of place, you don't know what you're doing. If your timing is spot on, you must know what you're doing because you're in control. They have no idea whether you could have shown them another swish pattern, or told them another fascinating story about a coaching session. All they know is that you say you'll cover X, Y and Z and finish at 4:00, and that's what you do.

When I run the assessment days, particularly for Practitioner, I walk around and keep an eye on things but I'm not really listening to the discussions, I'm more interested in whether the clients look happy. It's easy to say what I would have done instead of the Practitioner, what technique I would have chosen, what question I would have asked, but I'm not in their position, and because I'm walking from group to group, I'm not hearing every conversation in its entirety. Therefore, the only criteria for success that I really pay attention to is whether the sessions finish on time. If they do, then the Practitioner must have:

- Kept an eye on the clock

- Made a plan

- Adapted their plan to the time available

- Ended the session

It seems too simplistic, doesn't it? Yet if we look at the last in a sequence events and that's OK, then everything that came before must have been OK too. Now, if you're giving your learners feedback then you can't do this because by the time the session ends, it's too late to help them. Therefore, I don't give feedback because that would undermine the authority of the coach. I might make some notes for discussion at the end of the day, but I do not intervene during the assessment sessions. Well, if I saw a client in real distress and a Practitioner doing something to cause that then I probably would intervene by calling the Practitioner away. I've never had to do that, and it's important for the confidence of the Practitioners that they are free to do what they think is right in their coaching session. Importantly, any feedback does not take time away from the coaching session, so I tell them that they have 30 minutes and that's what they get.

Your plan means that your learners get what they paid for, and you get the satisfaction of giving them what you promised you would give them.

7.1.1.1   Success Criteria

What is the success criteria for your training? What is the measure that you are using to determine your performance?

How do you use this measure to continuously improve your performance?

7.2 Logistics

As a trainer, you're responsible for the organisation of the training event. You might be lucky to have assistants or administrators, but at the moment you stand up in front of your students, you become responsible for everything that happens. Therefore, you need to plan, not just for the learning but for everything that can make or break your students' experience.

I delivered a two day mentoring workshop for a corporate client in India recently. The room that the hotel gave us was far smaller than the one promised and, half way through the first day, maintenance engineers started banging and clattering in the ventilation system which opened into the room through a large grille above my head. I was worried that Tom Cruise was about to fall through it.

Shortly afterwards, the room began to fill up with toxic fumes. The hotel blamed decorators, but there didn't seem to be any decorating going on. To me, it smelt exactly like the street outside, so I figured that someone had set the ventilation system to draw in outside air, and within an hour the room was completely unusable. We were choking and our eyes were stinging.

How can your learners be expected to concentrate under such conditions?

I paused the training for an early lunch and asked the hotel manager move us, which he did, and everything was back to normal, or at least as normal as it can be in India.

7.2.1.1   Logistics and Your Learning Experience

What are the most important things to consider for the type of experience that you want to create?

Venue

Training room

Materials

Food and drink

Joining instructions

Support

7.2.2 Venue

If the venue is in a noisy location, or difficult to get to, or occupied by other conflicting groups, your learners aren't going to get the experience that you want for them. A venue might be cheap to hire, but if it's full of teenagers, or hosts a mother and baby group, or business people, or has the general public coming and going, your learners aren't going to feel comfortable. You also need to consider what other space is available for breakout groups, and how the weather might affect the use of the facilities.

7.2.3 Training room

If the room is too dark, or too small, or too hot, or too cold, your students won't be paying attention to you.

7.2.4 Materials

Are you providing learning materials? Printed notes? Books? Notepads? I've seen trainers give out horribly photocopied, stapled notes and school exercise books. What impression does that give to their learners?

If you find a good local printer, you might find that the cost of producing professional-looking notes is much less than you might think.

Another option, if you're running NLP Practitioner and Master Practitioner training, is that you can use the books that I've produced for that purpose. You can order them from me at 50% of the cover price, which may also be more cost effective than printing your own notes.

7.2.5 Food and drink

What are you providing for your learners? What do they need? What would make them comfortable?

Water is obvious. Hot drinks? Biscuits? Home made biscuits or cheap biscuits from the supermarket? What impression do these give your learners?

7.2.6 Joining instructions

Think about what you want to share with your participants ahead of your training. Obviously you'll share the logistics, location, running times and so on. How about letting them know what to bring with them, or what work to do in advance?

Remember that joining instructions are also an ideal way to get your learners into the right frame of mind before they arrive.

With what you've learned about NLP so far, you can easily think of how you can achieve that.

7.2.7 Support

Are you proving post-training support to your learners? Is it a modular course, and if so, what support do they get between modules? Will they have assignments to complete?

7.3 Learning Plan

Many people call themselves trainers when they're really not; they're subject matter experts at best. They are happy to stand up in front of a group and share the benefit of their experience, but that's not training. Remember, the purpose of training is to give people the knowledge and ability to do something specific. Impressing your learners with war stories might give them knowledge, but certainly not the ability to replicate what you're asking them to do. That isn't a training course, it's a presentation.

Good trainers always have a training plan which forms the skeleton of a learning event. A training plan will help you to:

- Deliver consistently

- Stay on schedule

- Cover everything that you intend to

Consistency is important because you need to make sure that all of your learners have the same experience and leave with the same knowledge and abilities, regardless of which session they attend. If you don't achieve that then you're treating your learners inequally, giving them a poor service and, most importantly of all, any evaluation becomes meaningless because the goalposts move with each learning event.

A training plan needs to be a very simple document so that you can easily keep track of where you are and where you're going in the training session.

How you write your training plan is really up to you, although it's a good idea to include at least the following information within a spreadsheet or table:

Time	Duration	Outcome	Method	Notes
You can quickly glance at the clock to check you're on time.	The duration of the training Step in minutes.	The outcome of the training Step	Delivery Method e.g. video, discussion, lecture, demo, game...	Any particular points to cover, quotes to share, handouts etc.
09:30	15	Learn each others' names	Name game	Covertly leads into the customer welcome.
09:45	15	Get into a customer mindset	Discussion - your experiences as a customer	

Remember, when you create your plan and deliver your training...

Don't aim for perfection

Aim for **consistency**

You cannot improve anything if you don't establish a consistent baseline. If you're perfecting a recipe, you can't succeed by changing all of the ingredients at the same time. If you do, it is by luck and you're unlikely to be able to reproduce it.

You cannot set out to improve anything, you can only change your actions. If you intend to improve something, you are trying to control the end result, which is impossible when other people are concerned. Therefore, you can never improve your training, you can only ever change your actions and measure the results of those new actions. Improvement is an outcome, an end result. It cannot be an intention, because until you make a change, you have no idea what will lead to an improvement. If you think that you do know, then you are guessing based on past experiences.

Consistency in your training delivery is absolutely the first and most important step in improving the results of your training. Once you have consistency, you can change small elements and measure the effect, and when you keep on doing that, the result will be the improvement that you're looking for.

7.3.1.1 Training Plan

Create a plan for the first hour of your Practitioner and Master Practitioner training.

On the next two double pages you'll find tables that you can use to write out the start of your training, which is of course the most important time, apart from the end. And all the bits in between.

Before you plan out your timetable for that first hour, give some thought to what you want to achieve at the start of your training; your opening statements, questions, stories and so on. How do you want to introduce your training? How do you want to influence your audience's state and expectations? Consider these points before starting your detailed plan.

Practitioner:

Master Practitioner:

Time	Duration	Outcome

Method	Notes	(Practitioner)

Time	Duration	Outcome

Method	Notes (Master Practitioner)

The NLP Trainer Training Manual

[8] Your NLP Training Plan

As a NLP Trainer, it helps if you actually know the techniques of NLP. Later in this book, I've included the SNLP certification criteria for Practitioner, Master Practitioner and Trainer so that you can see the standards that you will be assessing your students against.

You'll see that the criteria for a trainer really boil down to two things; being one step ahead of your students and knowing NLP inside out at the levels of Practitioner and Master Practitioner.

The easiest way to be one step ahead of your students is to have a well designed learning plan, and by that I mean a plan which follows some kind of flow and which allows you to cover the syllabus without having to rush. A good plan will keep you on track and on time, and that will keep the whole learning process under control.

Earlier, when I was talking about the art of performance, I said that, when you ask your students for someone to help with a demo, it helps if you start by asking the right question. I want you to work out what that is for yourself.

8.1.1.1   Selecting Your Subject

Work through the Practitioner syllabus and create a description for each technique which will select the person who will be the best demonstration subject for you.

For example, "I'd like someone to help me with a demo who has an instant reaction to something or someone that they would rather not have, and as soon as you've had that reaction, you kick yourself and promise yourself you won't do it again, yet you do, every time."

I've set aside the next few pages for you to do this.

Submodalities

Description to attract the right demonstration subject:

Your outcome for this part of your training:

What other parts of your training does this connect with?

How will you make those connections?

Anchoring

Description to attract the right demonstration subject:

Your outcome for this part of your training:

What other parts of your training does this connect with?

How will you make those connections?

Well Formed Outcomes

Description to attract the right demonstration subject:

Your outcome for this part of your training:

What other parts of your training does this connect with?

How will you make those connections?

Rapport

Description to attract the right demonstration subject:

Your outcome for this part of your training:

What other parts of your training does this connect with?

How will you make those connections?

Pacing & Leading

Description to attract the right demonstration subject:

Your outcome for this part of your training:

What other parts of your training does this connect with?

How will you make those connections?

Swish

Description to attract the right demonstration subject:

Your outcome for this part of your training:

What other parts of your training does this connect with?

How will you make those connections?

Squash

Description to attract the right demonstration subject:

Your outcome for this part of your training:

What other parts of your training does this connect with?

How will you make those connections?

Perceptual Positions

Description to attract the right demonstration subject:

Your outcome for this part of your training:

What other parts of your training does this connect with?

How will you make those connections?

Meta Mirror

Description to attract the right demonstration subject:

Your outcome for this part of your training:

What other parts of your training does this connect with?

How will you make those connections?

Milton Model

Description to attract the right demonstration subject:

Your outcome for this part of your training:

What other parts of your training does this connect with?

How will you make those connections?

Meta Model

Description to attract the right demonstration subject:

Your outcome for this part of your training:

What other parts of your training does this connect with?

How will you make those connections?

Eye Accessing Cues

Description to attract the right demonstration subject:

Your outcome for this part of your training:

What other parts of your training does this connect with?

How will you make those connections?

Strategies

Description to attract the right demonstration subject:

Your outcome for this part of your training:

What other parts of your training does this connect with?

How will you make those connections?

Collapsed Anchors

Description to attract the right demonstration subject:

Your outcome for this part of your training:

What other parts of your training does this connect with?

How will you make those connections?

Trance Induction

Description to attract the right demonstration subject:

Your outcome for this part of your training:

What other parts of your training does this connect with?

How will you make those connections?

Fast Phobia Cure

Description to attract the right demonstration subject:

Your outcome for this part of your training:

What other parts of your training does this connect with?

How will you make those connections?

Six Step Reframe

Description to attract the right demonstration subject:

Your outcome for this part of your training:

What other parts of your training does this connect with?

How will you make those connections?

Timeline

Description to attract the right demonstration subject:

Your outcome for this part of your training:

What other parts of your training does this connect with?

How will you make those connections?

9 Activity Design

I'm guessing that your training design won't be based solely on you standing in front of your students, lecturing to them. This style of training is, at the same time, both the most effective way to control what happens and the least effective way to create learning.

If you're an inexperienced trainer then you will have a tendency to lecture because you will have a tendency to focus on what you want to say.

As you gain more experience, your attention will shift to the experience that you are creating, and you will realise that listening is not much of an experience, and you will think more and more about what you want your learners to do so that they have experiences that they can reflect on and learn from. Great! So... what experiences? You'll have seen many different training exercises from your time at school up until now. You'll have seen some that just didn't engage you and some that did. What works to engage you is, of course, subjective, however that's the best place to start because if you're not doing something that interests and engages you then you've got no chance of engaging your students.

In The NLP Master Practitioner Manual, there's a chapter on the installation of models and a reference to isomorphism. If you want to train someone to perform a task, such as baking a cake, and you show them exactly how to perform that task then that is what they will be able to do. However, they won't be able to do anything else. They won't be able to make scones or bread, for example, because that's not what you've taught them. If your focus is on making as much money as possible from your students then you'll want to train them in very narrow skill areas so that they have to keep coming back to you. On the other hand, if you want to instil generative learning which enables your students to adapt their skills into new environments then you can teach them the underlying principles which they can then adapt into different situations or applications.

9.1.1 Isomorphic Exercises

An isomorphic exercise is one where a seemingly unrelated activity bears a structural resemblance to the model, thereby encouraging the learner to generalise their experience which embeds it more effectively and makes the learning accessible in a wider range of situations. When you deliver an isomorphic exercise correctly, you'll hear your learners say, "Ah! This is just like..."

For example, let's say that you want to install a model of complaint handling. One of the key steps in the model is the taking of notes, because it serves as a 'flow control' mechanism whilst also signalling to the complainant that you take their complaint very seriously.

Let's say that you want your learners to practice writing notes verbatim, because in complaint handling, it's very important to be factually correct and not change the complainant's words.

Make an audio recording of an angry complainant, speaking too quickly for the learners to write down their words. Put the recording on a computer or a tape so that the learners can control the conversation with the pause, rewind and play buttons. Focus their attention on the overt purpose of the exercise by having them check each other's transcripts and awarding points or prizes for the most accurate.

When you set the exercise up, position it only as a note taking activity, but when you later move onto a face to face interaction exercise, point out that taking notes, and the interpersonal skills required to do so, are the equivalent of the pause, rewind and play buttons. By practising first on the recording, you take away the stigma attached to interrupting the complainant and not wanting to appear rude or inflame the situation, and by then reintroducing the concept later on, the learners have already practised the mechanism. The learners will learn to take notes more effectively, because there was no interpersonal barrier of having to interrupt another person, as there would be in a pairs or group exercise. The learners are completely free to hone their note taking skills, and we'll add in the interpersonal skills later on.

This achieves the following outcomes which are each characteristics of the high performer's approach:

- Separate the flow control mechanism from the emotional stigma of interrupting the complainant

- Take notes to record the complainant's words verbatim

- Take notes to signal the complainant's importance

- Take notes to control the conversation, stick to the facts and prevent emotion from taking over

Now, you might wonder what makes an isomorphic exercise so special. After all, separating out the note taking from the interpersonal skills is logical, isn't it?

Firstly, how many trainers do you honestly think would separate the two? Isn't it more likely that most trainers would have the learners practice note taking with each other, because that's just easier?

Secondly, there are lots of ways that you could have your learners practice note taking. What is special is that you have chosen a practice exercise which uses a number of metaphors for the approach that you want them to take in handling a complainant. The metaphor works both ways; controlling the recording is 'like' controlling the complainant, and treating the complainant factually and objectively is 'like' pressing play, pause and rewind without worrying about how the tape recorder feels about it. When you install the complete model effectively, you don't have to install any incantations for reassuring the customer, such as "Your complaint is important to us", because the complaint handler demonstrates that the complaint is important. They don't need to signal to the complainant that they care, because their whole attitude to the interaction is one of concern and care. If you teach a disengaged, disinterested car salesperson to say, "So, can you see yourself..." then the harm caused by the incongruence far outweighs any statistical benefit of the incantation. A disinterested and sarcastic complaint handler will damage your business far more than the issue that the complainant is contacting you about.

Remember, of course, that a high performing complaint handler does not use their notes as a barrier, because that will frustrate the complainant further. The high performer uses their notes as an *enabler*. How do they achieve this subtle but vital difference? Because it's important that you understand that the tiny difference between the two means the difference between installing an effective model and creating a cargo cult with its rituals and incantations. The difference is that the high performer doesn't shut the complainant out while they take notes; they keep looking at them or talking to them. Their focus is on the complainant, not the notebook.

Good complaint handlers have an attitude which clearly signals:

- We're not perfect but we want to get better

- I'm grateful that customers make the effort to give me feedback rather going to our competitors

- We won't get it right every time

- My job is to listen, not to judge

- Without customers, we wouldn't have a business

- I will concentrate on the facts, hear all sides of the issue and put right what we've done wrong

- Some problems are outside of our control

- The customer is always right, but that doesn't mean they automatically get their own way

- One unhappy customer impacts our business more than a hundred happy customers

You can therefore design training exercises which are not a simple dry-run of the actual activity or task but are a metaphor for that task.

Much corporate training takes place in a classroom without real customers, and uses the 'role play' as a substitute for a customer interaction. This is worse than useless. Not only does the role play not reproduce a genuine interaction, it even teaches an idealised set of responses which will not reflect a real-life interaction.

In a role-play, the person playing the customer is given a briefing to follow, for example that they are the IT manager of ABC Software and they have an ongoing problem with the software crashing. The first problem is that the trainer who writes the role-play is not really an IT manager, so they write the briefing in a way which no real IT manager would relate to. Secondly, the learner playing the IT manager isn't an IT manager, and the briefing means even less to them. During the actual role-play, the learner has no depth of experience to draw upon and draws upon cliched phrases. Meanwhile, the learner who is practising the interaction does have a depth of experience because they're practising the execution of an aspect of their day-to-day work, such as customer service or sales. They know that the 'IT manager' is faking it and the entire role-play is a contrived facsimile of a real interaction.

What do the learners learn from all of this?

With an isomorphic exercise, all of the learners are equal, all have the same understanding of the exercise and the same foundation of prior knowledge. Your skill as a trainer is then in connecting the real-life requirements of the learners' jobs with the metaphors within the exercise.

Here are two examples of exercises that I often use in management and leadership training because they can be related to many different aspects of a manager's job, leading into a number of discussions which reflect on the activity from many different perspectives.

9.2 Giving Feedback

You'll be working in groups of three for this exercise.

Manager:

Place the target for your thrower to aim for. Don't let them see where you place it, and make it challenging but achievable. Do not move the target once you've placed it.

Give your thrower feedback on their performance with the objective of getting them to hit the target.

Thrower:

Stand with your back to the target.

Throw the paper ball over your shoulder, aiming for the target.

Don't look at the target!

Wait for feedback and then have another go.

Observer:

Make sure neither the manager nor thrower break the rules.

Note anything that you find interesting about the behaviour of either the manager or thrower.

9.3 Construction Time

In this exercise, you'll be competing in teams of 4 or 5 people for a prize.

A maximum of 30 minutes is allowed for the task.

Outside of the room is a model which you must reproduce using the parts supplied.

Only one member of a team can be out of the room at any time.

No writing materials, mobile phones, cameras, model parts etc. are allowed outside of the room.

You may not touch the model that is outside of the room and you may not interfere with the other team's model.

You may look at the model as much as you like.

Your team's score will be calculated as the time it took your team to finish your model, plus a 2 minute penalty for every piece not in the correct place.

The winning team will have the lowest total time.

Your team's time will be measured at the point at which you declare your model complete.

9.4 Activity Review

Look back over the previous two exercises and review what happened.

How do the rules of the exercise influence behaviour?

What learning processes could be observed in the exercises?

Looking at the exercises objectively, what would be the quickest way for someone to achieve the stated outcome of the task?

How can you build these exercises into a learning cycle?

How can you encourage your learners to step back and become aware of what they have learned at a more abstract level?

What are the most valuable questions to ask your learners to get them to arrive at the insights you want them to have?

9.5 Tips for the Exercises

9.5.1 Giving Feedback

When you first demonstrate the activity, open with a 'contrast frame', showing the audience the difference between different types of feedback. For example, ask the thrower to have a go and, assuming they miss the target, say, "You missed". You might even add, "You idiot" to further reinforce the stereotype of a bad manager.

In the 15 years that I've been using this exercise, I've rarely seen anyone work out the easy way to do it by themselves. What I've observed is that the throwers achieve the goal through luck rather than iterative improvement based on feedback. What almost no-one figures out explicitly is a language and a set of parameters for the task. For example, the simple parameter of what constitutes success is something that usually only gets discussed after a thrower tries to bend what they believe to be the rules. When the thrower and the manager have different definitions for success, you can imagine the confusion that ensues.

Often, the learners in a group will reach a point of frustration where they believe that, whatever they do, they can't hit the target, and they begin to give up. Once one subgroup does this, their change of focus will affect other subgroups and that has to be stopped otherwise your overall learning outcome will be affected.

9.5.2 Construction Time

When you judge the models you need to be able to move them next to the 'reference' model, so I use a flat base that has 3 or 4 interconnecting "towers' stacked on top of it. Sometimes I'll hide pieces almost out of sight within the towers. If a team doesn't get the foundation right then every higher piece will be out of place too.

You can make the time 20 minutes, you can allocate points instead of time penalties, it's up to you. Obviously you need to be on the ball with the stopwatch because when the team leader declares their model finished, there might only be seconds separating teams.

In fact, if a team is really being smart, they'll declare their model complete as soon as they hear the first team do so, because at that point they can no longer win on time and they might win on penalties.

And if a team is being really, really smart, they'll win by declaring themselves finished as soon as you tell them to start. However, in years of using this exercise, no-one has ever done this. It's far more likely that teams will become obsessed with perfecting the model and forget that they're long past any chance of winning.

I prefer to use children's building blocks for this because it's easier to judge the model without a debate over whether a piece is in the right place or not, however at a push, I was able to reproduce the exercise with folded pieces of paper and sticky notes.

9.5.2.1   Design an Activity

Choose a basic skill that you would want someone to develop, such as giving feedback, listening, delegating a task etc.

Break that task down into its component parts.

Choose one of those parts and find other examples of that specific ability or behaviour. For example, if the skill is listening, one of the parts might be taking time to set aside distractions. What would be another example of that? How about clearing a table before eating dinner? Or clearing a desk before working on something important?

Design an activity that relates to the metaphor.

Design a series of questions to set the opening frame for the activity.

Design a series of questions to reflect on the learners' experiences of the activity.

Link the activity back into the larger context that you are training.

10 Presenting

You have your learning plan and you know your subject. Now you need to stand and deliver.

Public speaking is one of the most important skills in business today. In fact, Dale Carnegie's excellent book 'How to win friends and influence people' grew from his public speaking lectures.

Almost everyone in a business has, at some point, the need to present – job information, project updates, at an interview or even at a friend's wedding. The difference between doing this easily and doing it with difficulty is immediate and obvious.

Presenting and training are very different, however both require that you are comfortable talking to an audience. A presentation is more likely to be a transmission to the audience, a training session is more likely to be interactive.

When I ask people what the purpose of their presentation is, they often answer, "To inform the audience". Well, you expect them to do something with that information, and that information is new to them. Doesn't that description fit 'training' too?

In both cases, the presenter wants the audience to do something as a result of the presentation.

If we start to look at the detailed behaviours and outcomes, we find that there's really not much difference between a presentation and a training session from the presenter's point of view.

How does it look from the learner's point of view? Well, do you go to a presentation to learn something? Probably, yes. Why would you choose to attend a presentation on a subject that you already familiar with? Maybe you go to a presentation to get very specific information, perhaps about a new product, or a project that you need to know about. You might even be part of a decision-making group and you're attending a presentation to find out what you need to know about the decision.

Why would you attend a training session? To learn a set of skills, or some factual knowledge such as the latest updates to healthy and safety law?

You probably expect to learn something at a presentation, and you probably expect a training session to be engaging. Again, there's so much crossover that it's really hard to clearly distinguish one from another.

Maybe an old-fashioned view of presenting is one of the presenter talking at the audience with no interaction. Most of my school lessons were like that, and I was supposed to remember it all. So again, the level of interactivity doesn't give us a clue. So let's assume that presenting and training are the same thing, at least as far as the presenter's outcomes and behaviours are concerned.

It's interesting that one of the most common problems presented by business coaching clients is a fear of public speaking. It seems that the ability to communicate with a group is simultaneously the most admired and most feared skill in business.

If we break presenting down into its basic behavioural elements, we need two skills; the ability to speak, and the ability to stand up. If you can do both of those at the same time, you're already making a good start.

Of course, you can stand up and talk at the same time – you do it every day. The difference must be in doing it in front of an audience and the good news is that this affects your perception, not your behaviour, and perception is much easier for you to change.

What can people who are already confident and accomplished speakers learn from this? The first thing is group influence. When you present, you are using a highly specialised form of communication that allows you to communicate the same information to a number of people so that they then take specific action as a result. If you are using presentations to inform or update people then send them an email instead. A presentation is a very powerful group influence tool, so use it wisely.

As with everything, the key to success is planning. How do you plan a presentation? Do you start with what you want to say, or with what you want the audience to do? Do you start by designing slides or by designing results?

In this chapter, we're working both on your group influence skills and on your ability to present with impact. Group influence skills include your ability to communicate using multiple layers of information to different people and to get those people to act in unison.

Storytelling is probably the most powerful group communication and influence tool that you can master. The good news is that you are already an accomplished and experienced storyteller, even if you didn't think you could describe yourself that way. When you tell a friend or partner about your day at work, or when you are telling a joke, you are using your natural storytelling skills to influence the state of another person. By refining and practising those essential skills, you will be able to engage an audience and influence their state so that they act in the way you want them to.

Whatever the situation, you are presenting because you want to, and because there is something that you want to achieve. Otherwise, why are you devoting your time and effort to it?

If you're not clear on your own outcome, what hope have you got of achieving anything? Firstly you have no idea what the audience wants, and secondly they will each want something different. Trying to give the audience what they want as your only outcome is a recipe for... well, what do you think?

What value does the presenter bring over the slides or notes? If the presentation is just about facts and figures, send the audience an email. Don't waste their time sitting through a presentation if you're not going to add anything to it. They are there because they want to see you present the information, interact, ask questions. If all they wanted was the data, they would look it up on a website.

So, let's get on with the show.

10.1   Modelling Excellent Presenters

A good place to start developing a skill is to find someone who has it and model it. Public speaking is such a commonplace activity that it is easy to find people who do it well and people who do it badly. Just turn on the TV or radio to find people giving speeches or press conferences, and notice what works well in terms of managing the audience's state towards a particular outcome.

Because we have seen so many public speakers, starting from when we first went to school, you already have all the information you need to be the most outstanding presenter right there between your ears. In your head is a model of excellence that we can draw upon for you to develop your skills. You already know what inspires you – the chances are that it will inspire other people too, because it will already be naturally congruent with your own style.

Think back to someone who you think of as being an exceptional presenter, trainer, teacher or performer. What do they do?

The answers that I typically get to this question include:

- Personable – can talk to people

- Makes you feel comfortable

- Not formal

- Good eye contact

- Relaxed manner

- Had a clear pathway, as if they had planned a journey for the audience

- Talks about things I could relate to

- Sets no boundaries on what I could or could not do

- Often the simplest (just stands up and chats)

- Gets everyone involved – interactive

- Enthusiasm – interested in what they're talking about

- Confident

- Not following the text book

- Uses humour

- Knew a lot about the subject

- Tells stories

And, since we're talking about NLP, I have to ask, "How do you know they are confident, or relaxed, or that they know a lot?"

When we start to dig a little deeper, we find the specific behaviours that constitute 'good presenting':

- Smile and make eye contact with the whole audience

- Access many different states to reinforce the message

- Have a clear outcome

- Tell stories (that's how you know they are knowledgeable)

- Choose to answer or deflect questions

- Finish on time or early (tells you they're in control)

This information is not rocket science. For years, presentation skills courses have been trying to get people to emulate these behaviours. Unfortunately, they try to do this by getting course delegates to consciously copy those behaviours, giving them too much to think about and making them even more nervous than when they started!

The approach we're taking here is to develop the states and beliefs that underpin those behaviours, so you don't have to think about them – they just come naturally.

This also raises an idea that is absolutely critical to your performance as a presenter or trainer. When you think about someone you have seen who is a great presenter, that person is not in the same room as you – they are in your head. In fact, the model that you have in your head is not a complete model of that person, it is only a model of their performance 'on stage'. Therefore, no matter how good or bad a presenter you think you are, you already have a model of exceptional performance in your mind. All we need to do is unlock that and transfer it into your behaviour.

10.2   Anxiety

A fear of public speaking is the single most common problem I am presented with in coaching. What I have found over the years is that the structure seems to fall into two broad categories. Some people start having an internal conversation with themselves whilst presenting and this creates conflict and distraction. Some people imagine that the audience is judging them badly.

In the first case, I find it's helpful to give people strategies for remembering their presentations easily without interrupting their flow. For example, if someone writes their presentation out as a script, they have to stop their flow in order to read the script. Instead, I would get them to draw their presentation prompts using pictures.

In the second case, when I ask what happens when they stand up in front of the audience they often say, "I imagine the audience is looking at me", to which I reply, "well, that's because they are!".

What is often happening is that the presenter is seeing themselves from the audience's point of view and noticing all of their faults. The Perceptual Positions technique is ideal in this situation.

10.2.1.1   Perceptual Positions For Presenters

Imagine yourself giving a presentation. In 1st position, you are standing at the front of the audience, seeing them, hearing them, hearing yourself, noticing what you feel.

Move to a 2nd perceptual position, sitting in the audience looking up at yourself. As you sit in the audience, look around you and then look at yourself at the front of the room. Notice what you see and hear, and notice how you feel.

Move to a 3rd perceptual position as a neutral observer, at the back of the room or perhaps looking in through a door or window. Notice the way that 'you' in the audience interacts with and responds to 'you' at the front of the room.

Move back through 2nd position and finally into 1st position, taking with you anything you have noticed or learned.

Taking in what you noticed in the 3rd and 2nd positions, what seems different as you deliver your presentation now?

At this stage, most people will observe that the audience had far more important things to think about than the presenters minor habits and mistakes. And from the 3rd position, it all seemed quite distant and unimportant. Back in 1st position, most people will feel more of a balance in their relationship with the audience. Yes, the audience is looking at them, but they're not making as harsh a judgement as the presenter is making of themselves.

10.3   Getting Ready

If you ever worry or are nervous about a presentation, here are some very simple tools you can use to change that.

The first, and most important thing to remember is that the majority of people inadvertently make all kinds of everyday activities difficult, and these same people could make those same activities incredibly easy with just one simple, small adjustment.

Most people plan for the start of things, not the end

Public speaking, cold calling, going to the dentist and flying can be difficult for some people. How many times have you felt nervous about doing any of these? How many times have you felt nervous at the end? What many people experience is worry leading up to the event, nervousness at the start and relief at the end. Which of those three states would you like to feel, all the way through? Do you want to worry about it or look forward to it?

Let's look at the process of worry:

Imagine a future event	>	Imagine it turning out **badly**	>	Act as if it's happening now

The processes of worry and excitement are the same, with just a tiny change in content:

Imagine a future event	>	Imagine it turning out **really well**	>	Act as if it's happening now

So, here's the simple way that you can overcome doubt, worry, anxiety, nerves or fear:

Plan for the end!

So, when you imagine the presentation, imagine it from the point where you're saying thank you, the audience is nodding approvingly and you feel good about having done your best.

If you're having trouble accessing a resourceful state, here's a simple method you can use.

10.3.1.1   Anchoring a Presentation State

Firstly, think of the specific state you want to access. "Confident" is too vague, it isn't a state anyway, and overconfidence can be as harmful as nervousness.

Remember a specific time when you were in your chosen state. Remember what you saw, how bright the memory is, how sharp, how near, how big and how colourful. Next, remember what you heard, how loud, from where, how clear. Finally, remember what you felt, where, how warm or cold, how heavy or light, what movement, what sensation.

Make the picture bigger and brighter, the sounds louder and the feelings more intense as you double the feeling, and double it again. Say a word to yourself that represents this feeling and keep on repeating it as you concentrate on the feeling.

As you say the word to yourself and concentrate on your feelings, add a colour that seems relevant. See it washing over you and running through you, intensifying your state as it flows.

10.3.1.2   Owning the Space

Step into the presentation space at the front of the room and allow the audience to hand control of the room over to you. Just take a moment to notice how it feels and what thoughts are in your mind. Notice how the audience really looks, rather than only seeing what you had expected to see.

Stay there for slightly longer than feels comfortable.

When you get back to your chair, make a note of how you felt and what you noticed.

10.4   Setting the Scene

What do audiences want to know? What meanings should all presentations convey regardless of topic or content?

- I'm telling the truth

- You can trust me

- This is important to you

- This is relevant to you

- I really believe in this

- You're going to love this!

It might be useful to think about the high level message that runs through you presentations, and to consider that first when you are planning a presentation. If you get that in place, everything else you do has a strong foundation to build on.

10.5   Your Context

Take a moment to set your own personal context for presenting with impact – is it to clients, colleagues or someone else? Are you selling, persuading, informing or something else?

You might think that your job is to 'train' your audience or to 'teach' them, that is not the case. That is the means by which you are doing your job. Your job is actually to run a training business, or to be employed as a trainer, or whatever you are actually paid for. Remember, in any job, you are paid for your time, so whatever your activities are during your working hours, that's your job.

Think about the higher purpose that you are fulfilling by training people. What are you contributing to a business or community?

It's also worth thinking about what the audience expect from you. Do they expect an expert, or just a different perspective? Do they expect a hero or a fall guy?

10.6   Planning Outcomes

If you don't want your audience to do anything as a result of your presentation then you are wasting your time and theirs. An email could replace your presentation if all you want to do is transmit information. You could simply send your learners a book or your training handouts to read. Why make them sit though hours of you prattling on if you're only reading out what the notes say anyway? What value are you adding?

1 What do you want from this training?
2 How will you know when you have it?
3 What will having it do for you?
4 What will having it do for your clients and colleagues?
5 What do you need in order to get it?
6 What can the rest of us do today to help you get this?
7 What stops you from achieving this now?
8 What can you imagine yourself doing differently?

Even a decision or an opinion is an action because it requires the audience to process information and then do something. Forming an opinion is an active process, just as much as buying a product.

- What do I want?

- How will the people in this room help me to get it?

- What do I need them to do for me?

- What state do they need to be in to achieve that?

When you create a Well Formed Outcome for your presentation, you'll know it has to be under your control. If you want the audience to understand or agree, that's not under your control, so first you have to know what it is you want.

10.6.1.1 Your Outcome as a Trainer

Form your own outcome before you think about your audience.

Positive
Under your control
Real – what you can see, hear, feel
Ecological

Many people tell me that they present in order to 'inform' or 'educate'. That's not under your control!

If we work outwards in layers of control, the first thing that is under your control is your own state. When you're in rapport with the audience, your state will influence their state and their state will make it easier for them to achieve the outcome you want for them.

Aside from all the influencing tricks you could learn, the simplest way to get people to do what you want is to tell them what you want. It's important to get into the habit of telling people clearly what you want and what you need from them.

10.6.1.2   Ask For What You Want

"What I want is"

"What I need from you is"

"How do you feel about that?"

The final question, a 'tag question' just pushes the outcome home as it tends to elicit an agreeable response in the majority of helpful, reasonable people. The important thing is that it elicits a response – because you do want a responsive audience, don't you?

If you ask for something that people can't give you, they will tell you – either by saying "no" or by saying "erm...OK" whilst looking like they mean 'no'.

I've noticed that many people convert the last question into, "What do you think about that?" or "Is that OK?"

We don't care about what the audience think. We want to know how they feel, because we want them to be aware of how they feel. We are also not asking their permission. So the original wording of the question is important.

Many people are afraid to ask for what they want. That's OK, because if everyone asked for what they want, there would be too much noise. It's good that many people are brought up by their parents to believe that accepting second best, accepting what they're given is somehow a good thing. This means that it's very easy to get what you want, just by asking for it. It's precisely because other people are afraid to do it that it works so nicely.

And you're not afraid to get what you want, are you?

Of course, there is another explanation. Imagine for a moment that the world is full of people who are reasonably happy, well intentioned, kind and helpful. They want to help you, as long as what you're asking for doesn't specifically disadvantage them. They want to help you, but they don't know how. So by telling them what you want, you are helping them to help you, which makes them happy.

After all, you feel happy when you've helped someone, don't you?

"What I want is for you to think about how this is important for your business, so what I need you to do is pay attention and ask any questions that help you to understand how we can work together, how do you feel about that?

Years ago, I worked with a client who had problems with internal communication. They had a board meeting every two months where they would cover all of their project updates and make all of their important decisions. The meeting essentially comprised two days of presentations.

What was happening was this: someone would present a project update and at the end certain people would start asking awkward questions, saying they had forgotten something, questioning their approach, saying they should do something different, generally picking the project apart and making the presenter feel like they were under attack. The presenter would exclaim "but all of this was in the agenda, didn't you read it?" Of course, no-one ever did read the agenda. They were too busy.

Someone else would present some information for a decision – something simple like buying mobile phones. They would go through tariffs, figures, suppliers and so on, and at the end of the presentation as the board to make a decision. More questions. "Have you talked to that supplier?", "Why are you doing it that way?", "Why don't you talk to this supplier?", "Why are you looking at those phones?", "What's the cost of calling another mobile on that one?". The presenter would exclaim "but all of this was in the agenda, didn't you read it?" Of course, no-one ever did read the agenda. They were too busy.

And meeting after meeting, decisions didn't get made, projects didn't move forwards and everyone learned to feel a sense of dread when it was time for the next meeting.

The solution was very simple, and I bet you can guess what it was. The presenters weren't telling the audience how to listen, they weren't telling the audience what they needed to do. So each person in the audience settled into their default role – to fall asleep, or to challenge, or to show that the presenter hadn't really thought it through, or whatever it was.

It didn't help that the presentations were all jumbled together, so the audience would never really understand what the point of the next one would be. It's no wonder they were confused and just retreated to their comfort zones.

What I had them do instead was begin each presentation with a framing statement, such as:

"Here is an update on my project, I don't need any advice or feedback at this stage, it's for your information only"

"I'm going to present information about the mobile phone purchasing project, and at the end I want you to tell me which supplier you think we should use"

Saying, "Here is an update on my project, I don't need any advice or feedback at this stage, it's for your information only" tells people exactly what is expected of them. Conversely, presenting a huge volume of facts and figures and only then asking people to make a decision is simply asking for trouble. If you tell people up front what you expect, they will pay attention in the right places and be able to make a decision when you need them to, instead of saying they need more time to think or asking difficult questions just to divert attention away from the fact that they weren't listening.

Of course, you could do even better than this. You could make sure your presentation is even more focused and impactful. Using the examples above:

"I'm here to give you an update on my project. What do you need to know in order to feel comfortable updating your own teams on our progress?"

"I'm asking you to make a decision on which mobile phone supplier we use. What information do you need from me to make that decision?"

10.7   When Does the Presentation Start?

When do you think a stage play or musical begins? When the actors first speak their lines? In the music that is playing before the show starts? Upon entering the theatre, even? The answer is that it starts the moment you buy your ticket.

When does a night out with friends start? As you walk into the bar? As you're getting ready? As you're getting ready to leave work?

When does your holiday start? When you step off the plane? Or when you book it?

Why is this? Because as soon as you start to think about something like a night out, or a holiday, or a presentation, you are building a simulation of it in your mind. As soon as you make the decision, your mind begins preparing you for it. That preparation might include wondering who will be there, thinking about what might happen, feeling excited, thinking about what you want to learn, thinking about how to get there.

We survive by predicting the future. Our ability to catch balls and trains requires the future to be much the same as the past, so we create generalised rules that apply over time. The problem is that we predict the future based on past events, and as the people who manage your investments say, that is a very risky approach.

It's a completely natural, human process, and by being aware of it, you gain greater control.

You will be communicating with your audience long before you stand up to speak to them, so it's very important that you start shaping their expectations to support your outcome.

If you ask, many people will say that the presentation starts when they stand up to speak.

This is unhelpful for two reasons:

- It puts even more focus on the act of standing up, which is the bit most people avoid

- It loses a huge opportunity to influence the audience and set their expectations

Invitation setup	Room setup	Presentation	Q&A	Close

What communication do you have with the audience before the presentation that you can use to reinforce your presentation?

Do you send out an agenda? A joining pack? An email? Each of these is an opportunity to prepare the audience for your presentation so that you have a much greater chance of achieving what you want from it.

If you tell the audience what to expect, they will adjust their ability to pay attention accordingly.

If you don't they will pay attention to whatever fits their preconceived expectations, which means you will get random results at best.

Set the audience's expectations as soon as you begin communicating with them.

As you stand up, you step into an imaginary space at the front of the room, created by the audience. The existence of an audience presupposes the existence of a presenter – and so you are stepping into a role that is waiting for you to claim it.

As you step into that space, you take control of the room, and you do not under any circumstances give control back to the audience until you are ready to.

When you're delivering training, you have a perfect opportunity to begin influencing your learners through the joining instructions that you'll send them.

10.8   Planning States

What will be the state of your audience? Open minded? Impatient? Confrontational? Complacent? Nervous? Afraid? Curious?

Many presenters just launch in and start talking at the audience instead of first tuning themselves into the audience's state.

Begin by thinking about the audience's starting state. Then, thinking about the desired outcome for the presentation, choose a useful end state for the audience. Finally, plan a route.

10.8.1.1   Plan a State Journey

1 Start state:
2:
3:
4:
5 End state:

It is very important to be realistic about the audience's start state. You might want them to be curious, but if the reality is that they are tired and bored then you can take that into account. Remember; their start state is neither good nor bad, it's just the way that it is, and it has nothing to do with you.

Their start state will depend not just on what has happened to them prior to the presentation, but also on their expectations of the presentation itself based on their previous experiences. This is a very important point too, and illustrates the importance of knowing when the presentation starts.

You will probably recognise this as an extension of the concept of pacing and leading, and you'll remember that the first stage of pacing is to gain rapport. If the audience is feeling critical, there's no point pretending they are curious. First you need to pace their critical state in order to lead them out of it. How do you do that? Come on! Do you want me to come and do the presentation for you?

Get their attention

Tell them what to do

Give them the
Information
they need

Get them to do it

Presenters who don't have the advantage of this approach often start by planning what they want to say rather than how they want the audience to respond. This is why their presentations seem more like transmissions than interactions.

What about technical presentations? Surely they serve to inform or instruct the audience? Again, what do you want them to do with that information? Agree with it? Make a decision? Understand it? Use it? Misuse it?

The outcome for the audience is always your starting point for designing a presentation. Once you know this, the rest is easy.

10.9   What the Audience Wants

What do audiences want to know? What meanings should all presentations convey regardless of topic or content?

Are there some silent, hidden questions that the audience need answering before they can begin to listen? You know there are. They're the same questions that you were asking as we started this workshop.

As you begin your presentation, the people in the audience have these questions rattling around in their minds. They are probably not consciously aware of them, yet they still need to be answered.

They are questions like:

- Do we have anything in common?

- Do I like you?

- Do I trust you?

- Do I believe you?

- Do you believe you?

- Do you know what you're talking about?

- Is this relevant to me?

- Do I respect you?

There may be other questions too, depending on the situation.

How do you know that you like someone? Is it because they say "You can like me" or is it something else?

It might be useful to think about the high level message that runs through you presentations, and to consider that first when you are planning a presentation. If you get that in place, everything else you do has a strong foundation to build on.

By giving the audience the opportunity to find the answers to these questions first of all, you will ensure their full attention later on. It really is worth investing time in this, because that investment will pay off greatly later on, as you will soon discover.

10.10   Environment

Bear in mind that the environment you're presenting in will greatly influence the audience and your outcomes, particularly if you plan the environment in conjunction with the audience's expectations.

You can think not only about the venue and room but also branding and signs which add to the expectations of the audience.

You can also think about things like refreshments, using a lectern and so on. If you stand behind a lectern, you will lose rapport with the audience because they can't see you. If you have water available, you can use it to give yourself time to think about questions.

The environment can support or hinder you in achieving your outcome, so it's worth taking some time to think about it.

10.11   Structuring the Presentation

There are a number of formats that you can use to establish communication with the audience. Here are a few ideas for you to practice. Remember that success, in NLP terms, doesn't mean thinking about what will work and ruling out what you think won't – it means that you do everything and notice what really works!

10.11.1   Framing

By telling people what you want them to do, you are helping them to filter the information so that they pay attention to what is important for them. If you don't tell people what to do until the end, they will be completely unprepared for it and will not do what you ask. This process is called labelling or framing, and it's often used naturally by anyone who is a skilled communicator.

- I'm going to present a project update after which I'd like you to give me feedback.

- I'm going to present a proposal to you after which I'd like you to make a decision.

- I'm going to show you a demonstration after which I'd like you to practice a coaching technique

10.11.2   Outcome Focus

There's an old saying used by old presentation skills trainers: tell them what you're going to tell them, tell them, then tell them what you've told them. In other words, the audience have a limited attention span so you have to drum your message into them. Here's an updated version, for a more modern audience:

- Tell them what you want them to do

- Present the information they need in order to do it

- Tell them what you want them to do

10.11.3   Association (Shifting Referential Index)

Begin talking about the wider context, people in general, then move to a more relevant section of the population, then to the people in the room, then to 'you' and finally to 'I'. Throughout the sequence, the referential index shifts as follows:

Everyone (everything) > them > us > you > I

10.11.4   Timeframe (General Backtrack Pacing)

Begin at some point in time before the present moment, listing all the shared experiences up until the present moment to elicit and agreement state, then continue forward in time to gain commitment to a course of action.

10.11.5   Frame/Story/Question

Frame the communication to direct the audience's attention, tell a short story and then ask a question to shift the audience's state and refocus their attention.

10.11.6   Pacing Current Experience

The first thing you need to achieve in your presentation is to get the audience's attention. You can ask questions, tell them about yourself, use an ice breaker, tell a joke, or do anything else that fits the context.

One very useful way to achieve this is to build your audience towards an 'agreement state' in which they are more likely to agree with you, consider your ideas favourably and make the decisions you want them to make.

So, right now, you're reading these words and you might think about your next presentation. Perhaps you've presented in the past, or experienced other people presenting to you. In either case, you may be the kind of person who really wants to achieve the best you can and refine the skills you're already developing. It's good that you're taking such an active interest in yourself because you know the results that it will bring you.

Was there anything in that last paragraph that you could disagree with? Was there anything to agree with?

In the first section we talked about pacing the audience's state. This is the same process, and this time you're pacing their experience. As you begin with very general facts that are true for the audience, you will see them nodding in agreement. As your presentation becomes more specific, or less factual, they will be more likely to agree with you than to disagree. For example, to say that you're reading about presentation skills is true. To say that you're reading the best way to develop your presentation skills is a belief. Your beliefs - product benefits, opinions or proposals - are more likely to be accepted if your audience is in an agreement state.

When practising hypnosis, we use a simple script that rotates the client between their external experience and their internal focus:

10.11.6.1   Cycling Focus

Tell your partner three things that you know they can see/hear/feel

Tell your partner one thing that may be true - a suggestion

Ask your partner what they are aware of

Repeat 4 or 5 times

10.11.6.2   Leading Learning

Tell the audience three things that are true now or are shared experience

Tell the audience one thing that may be true - a suggestion

Ask the audience for their agreement

And you might still be wondering what this has to do with presenting, so here are a couple of examples, starting with something that I hear at almost every sales conference.

- It's been a tough year

- Competition has been intense

- We've worked hard

- Your targets are doubling next year

- Leadership is key to business success

- Effective leaders inspire their staff

- Leaders can be both born and bred

- Peter Freeth develops your leadership potential

It's always useful to have your audience in an agreeable state before you start transmitting information at them. This simple technique is a very powerful way to lead the audience into an agreeable state by telling them things that are true – either in their experience or in the present moment, for example:

- You have all travelled to be here today

- We are all together

- You can hear me

- You can take a moment to be comfortable

- We have some presentations before lunch

- Some of you might be curious

- Some of you may already know

- I know that you may be wondering

- You might be wondering, "what do I do with this?"

And of course, when the audience is in an agreeable state, they are more likely to agree with you.

10.11.7   Chunk Size

You can start at a high level of detail and work down throughout your presentation, giving the audience the opportunity to 'tune in' when you reach their preferred level of detail.

Tell the audience the purpose of your presentation, what you want to achieve and what they need to do to help you.

Start with background, big picture, landscape, 'true' information. Talk about the wider context to your presentation, both what's good and what's missing from it.

Move onto the detail of your presentation, what you are presenting, what problems it solves, what it achieves, how that helps the audience, what it does for them.

Summarise the key points, information, benefits, outcomes. Tell the audience what you want to achieve and what they need to do to help you.

10.12   Timing

It's more important to stick to time than to say everything you want to say. The audience will be left with a far better impression if they feel the presentation is complete than if there is any sense of something being left out.

As a rule of thumb, when you plan your presentation content, create enough content to fill about three quarters of your allocated time. The rest of that time will most certainly be taken up by late starts, questions, conversations and all the other unexpected things that happen whenever you work with children, animals or NLP students.

It is very easy to fill in time during a presentation, and by finishing early you give the impression of being very much in control - something that the audience will notice and appreciate.

If you have any activities or interactive sessions planned for your presentation, build in even more contingency, so that you create content for only half of the allocated time.

Many people take the approach that they have a lot to say about themselves and their companies, and it's very hard to pack all that into a short time. Certainly, if you believe that the function of a presentation is for you to tell the audience something, or give them information, then you will certainly find it difficult to pack in everything you have to say.

Let's take a different approach - one that takes a lot of pressure off you and makes the whole experience far more enjoyable. Simply ask yourself this question:

What one question can I ask that will get the audience to do what I want them to do?

After that, the only remaining question is what to do to pad out the remaining time!

If your set up and invitations have done their job, the audience already knows why they are there and what they need to do what they are there for. If someone asks you to make a decision, you already know what information you need. You don't have to sit through a comprehensive presentation of information which is very useful, it's just not useful for you. If the audience needs only some very specific information in order to take action, why waste time?

Here are some examples:

- What one thing would mean the most to you, to gain from this presentation?

- What information will be most useful to you right now?

- What can we do in this next hour that will make this whole presentation worthwhile?

Starting from the point of cramming in everything there is to say is difficult. Starting from the point of what your audience needs to hear in order to take the next step is easy.

So, here is a useful idea for you. Always start your presentations with a question:

What would you most like to hear about that will be most helpful or useful for you right now?

By concentrating on the answer to that question, timing will never be a problem for you.

10.13 Language Patterns

You can try out some different forms of language to find out the effect they have on the audience. Here are some examples.

10.13.1 Presuppositions

All language contains unspoken elements which must be accepted as true in order for the language to make grammatical sense. You can use this constructively, for example:

"When you buy a service like mine, what do you normally expect?"

The question is about customer expectation, but it makes no grammatical sense if the listener does not buy 'a service like mine'.

How about, "By fully engaging in this learning process, what do you hope to achieve?"

10.13.2   Reframes

Reframing can be used to change the meaning of information, for example, if the price of a product is high you can reframe that information to mean the price is an indication of exclusivity.

You can respond to even the most pointed objection or question with, "Excellent! What a great question", because it's important to recognise the value of the person even if their question may be inappropriate, which you'll recognise as one of the Presuppositions of NLP.

In coaching, you can use reframes to change the meaning of problems. I was recently asking a client to use their creativity to come up with options for a problem. One option was, "Move to a planet orbiting Mars" and my reply was, "Excellent! Your creative side is working really well!"

Whatever your audience does or says is good because it shows they are engaged. If they fall asleep, that's good too as they'll be easier to influence. You can't lose!

10.13.3   Embedded Commands

These are instructions that sit within a language structure that is not itself a command. Often, analogue marking is used to draw unconscious attention to the command. The simplest embedded commands are questions, which also take the form of presuppositions:

Can you let me know when you're ready to **pay attention** and begin?

What would you like to know that will really help you to **open up and engage** in this process?

And they can also be more complex:

I know that sometimes it seems difficult to **make a decision**, yet when you realise **you're in the best place** you just have to **go for it** and **trust yourself** to **do the right thing** for you.

The embedded commands are marked out using a gesture or vocal stress or even a pause, in exactly the same way that you would naturally stress important points in any conversation. However, with embedded commands, you're not necessarily placing the emphasis in the 'usual' places, and you therefore need to practice this technique.

10.13.4   Milton Model Language

Milton Model language is a framework within which the listener can insert their own meaning. It is very powerful in situations where you have to address the needs of interests of many different people, for example:

"You may have heard about this before or it may be new to you, in either case you might already be thinking about how to use this information and to learn even more before you make the right decision for you."

Milton Model is not a means of commanding your students to do your evil bidding. It is a means of communicating personally and specifically with every member of even the most diverse audience. Sometimes, people from many different backgrounds can attend the same training course, and while they each have their own particular interests and needs, there is of course one thing which drew them all together, here, right now, and when you speak to that need, you open up a whole new channel of communicating with each and every one of them.

10.14   Critical Filters

We each have a critical filter which evaluates incoming information to judge it against our own beliefs and perception of the world.

The filter is useful because it protects us from other people's beliefs. Unfortunately, it also prevents us from accepting new information too.

This means that if you present by talking facts at your audience, it doesn't matter how true or well researched you think those facts are, some people in the audience will find them contentious, simply as a result of the way you have presented them.

Fortunately, we can bypass this filter quite easily. Firstly, you can make sure that the people you're presenting to are in as receptive a state as possible before you begin presenting. How? Come on – you can remember!

- Using every opportunity to communicate with the audience prior to the presentation

- Framing the presentation so the audience know what to do

- Answering the audience's unspoken questions

Secondly, you can use the two forms of communication which will bypass the critical filter.

10.14.1   Questions

Why do questions bypass the
critical filter?

How do questions bypass the
critical filter?

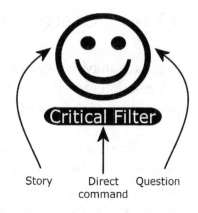

Questions don't convey any
information or instructions, do
they?

A structure of language which you hear as a question puts
you into a certain frame of mind, ready to search for an
answer. Over time, the right balance of questions will guide
your audience into a receptive, open minded state.

We hear questions when:

1. The speaker's voice pitch and eyebrows rise towards
    the end of a sentence, not to be confused with a
    stereotypical Australian accent which is different

2. A sentence starts with a word such as why, when,
    where, how, what, which, who, if, is, could, would,
    might, may, can

3. A statement ends with a tag question, such as
    couldn't it?, don't they?, do we?, can it?

After all, it's rarely wise to position yourself as a the
absolute expert who is going to give the audience all the
answers. It's generally useful to think of your role as being
to help the audience to explore the questions, and for them
to formulate their answers. As you'll see later, people rarely
ask a question in order to get a straight answer.

And in any case, an answer is rarely as simple as it seems. We ask questions because the answers mean something, not because they're plain facts. There is no such thing as a plain fact.

Consider these facts:

- 30 mph

- 2%

- 2 metres

How do you feel about them? Good? Bad? Indifferent?.

You see, in themselves they don't mean anything, but in context they can generate strong emotions. How about:

- Someone driving at 30 mph in a 20 mph area past a school at 8:30 am

- Being stuck behind someone driving at 30mph in a 60 mph zone when you have to catch a train

So questions not only bypass the audience's critical filters – they have the power to elicit very strong emotional responses.

10.14.2   Narrative Communication

Listen to a conversation and you will hear a combination of:

- Belief statements – which might sound like facts

- Questions – for many different reasons

- Narrative – which adds characters and sequence

This is a very important point. Human beings communicate with each other in a narrative. We don't communicate using factual statements, such facts are linked by a narrative, which includes characters – who did what to whom – and a sequence in time, so that we can recreate the situation mentally.

The simplest sentence will contain a subject, a verb and an object, and that is a story in itself.

As a person is talking, anyone listening is translating the words back into the original sensory experience. Of course, they can't translate it into exactly the original, so they are substituting their own experiences and references in order to make sense of it.

Firstly, this means that the more narrative you use, the easier you are to listen to.

Secondly, it means that the richer your narrative, the more vivid are the pictures you create in your audience's mind.

And thirdly, when I ask people on workshops what qualities they associate with excellent presenters, one which always comes out is that the presenter knew a lot about their subject. And when I ask how they knew that the presenter knew a lot – they told stories.

So storytelling is vital, it's natural, you already do it and to be an excellent presenter you can do more of it, purposefully. Right now, you communicate in many ways that already fit this form, including:

- Anecdotes

- Case studies

- Reports

- Any description of an event

10.15   Framing Your Communication

Effective communicators use a technique called 'framing', in which they direct your attention before they tell you the important bit, so you don't miss it. For example,

- I'm going to present some information after which I'd like you to give me your opinion.

- I'm going to present a project update after which I'd like you to give me feedback.

- I'm going to present a proposal to you after which I'd like you to make a decision.

By telling people what you want them to do, you are helping them to filter the information so that they pay attention to what is important for them. If you don't tell people what to do until the end, they will be completely unprepared for it and will not do what you ask.

10.16　Question-Story-Question

Instead of starting your presentation with a grand opening statement, why not start with a simple question?

Imagine you're at a conference. You meet with someone who you would dearly love to work with. You say, "What one thing could we show you today that would make the whole conference worthwhile?" Whatever they say, that's what you talk about. The entire presentation, centred around the one idea that will make the biggest difference to them.

Ask someone a **question** and, even for a moment, they are hooked. They are instantly put into a receptive frame of mind. After that, it's up to you to put their attention to good use.

Your **story** contains all of the facts and emotional content that provides a context for the question.

Asking your opening **question** again now causes the audience to formulate a new answer which is set in the context of your story.

The two **Questions** are hooked together by a **Story**:

The idea is very simple. Begin by posing the question. After leaving it to hang in the air for a few moments, move straight into your presentation. Do not obviously refer back to your opening question. At the end of your presentation, repeat the question. The content of your presentation has provided the answer, and the audience knows what to do.

Question	Subject
"What would you give to be able to correct one mistake in your life?"	A project to support disadvantaged teenagers
"How would you feel if you could save one more life today?"	Funding for a safety program
"How would you feel, knowing that you had changed the world today?"	Investment in something that will save energy or lives

Here's an example script.

> "What would you give to be able to correct one mistake in your life?
>
> I run a project for teenagers who have been in trouble with the police. Typically, they struggled at school, dropped out and got into the wrong company. Through peer pressure, which I know we've all felt in one way or another, they end up making a mistake that they regret for the rest of their lives. Through our project, that I'm seeking your support with, we help these teenagers to put right that mistake and to make sure it doesn't

take away their chance of a normal life, the kind of life that it's easy for people like us to take for granted.

I'm asking for your sponsorship, your time, your brand or just your funding. Which you give is up to you, all are invaluable to us and to the teenagers who are going to benefit so much from your help.

After all, what would *you* give to be able to correct one mistake in your life?"

The question takes on a different meaning as a result of what you say in the main body of the presentation, because the second question is now set in a new context.

10.16.1.1 Question-Story-Question

Practice this structure – write a short note against each part to remind yourself:

- Setting a frame – with a question

- Telling a story

- Asking a question

This is totally different to explaining what the story is about, because that destroys the power of the story, and you must never ever explain a story after you have told it. When you communicate in this narrative way, you create a vivid experience in the mind of the listener who then determines a subjective meaning from it. If you the explain the story, your meaning will be different to theirs, and the disagreement breaks rapport and distances the audience from you, undoing the good work you have done by telling the story in the first place.

For example, the 'right' way to do this: "Have you noticed how site safety is back in the news lately? Recently, when we were interviewing construction workers, I was surprised to find that..."

And the 'wrong' way: "Now I'm going to tell you a story about how important site safety is to construction workers. In a recent survey, 58% of respondents indicated... and what that means is..."

10.17   Nested Loops

Hypnotic change stories can come in the form of a nested loop, where a suggestion is embedded within another story. A format using two nested stories looks like this:

Start story 1	Start story 2	Suggestion	End story 2	End story 1

Nested loops can be complex to set up and require rehearsal, yet can be very powerful when used well.

Of course, the entire learning process is a series of nested loops, building every learning experience upon what came before and connecting to what comes beyond.

Without these connections, your training content will tend to fit into discrete 'boxes' and your learners will tend to lose a sense of connection between those areas of content.

For example, in training NLP, if you teach every technique as a separate skill without connecting those techniques together, your students will have a selection of techniques to choose from but may struggle to improvise and combine techniques, and may not see those techniques within the bigger frame of a client interaction.

Kolb's learning cycle is, obviously, a never ending loop rather than a series of discrete, unconnected cycles. You don't have a learning cycle today, then another one tomorrow. Your life is an ongoing cycle of experiencing, integrating and acting upon your sense of reality.

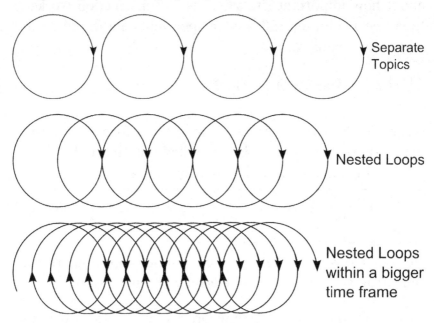

Separate Topics

Nested Loops

Nested Loops within a bigger time frame

Giving a story a nice, neat conclusion where all of the loose ends tie together might seem like a good idea, however there is a risk that for your learners, the story will end at that point, and what you're actually aiming to do, I hope, is continue that story of learning and self development beyond the training and into their lives.

How you achieve that can be very quick and very easy – simply linking back to what came before and suggesting what may come next.

When you're designing a training program, your content areas can link together in this same way. If you consider NLP Practitioner training, you'll find that a technique such as anchoring is part of every other technique, so if you treat anchoring as a distinct subject, you're greatly minimising the learning opportunity.

When I see NLP Practitioners who simply cannot anchor effectively, I know that they've been trained anchoring as a standalone technique for accessing a state. This is a trivial use of anchoring, it is far more valuable as a means of controlling the client's responses during the performance of other techniques. For example, in the Fast Phobia Cure, if you can't anchor the progressive dissociations, you find that your clients keep flipping into the associated memory and will be unable to change the submodalities of that memory and consequently will fail to experience a change in their subjective experience of the 'problem'.

Instead, when you link anchoring through all of the other techniques, you give your students multiple opportunities to practice, they develop a high level of skill through that practice and they become much more confident with all of the other techniques.

10.18   Reframing

Reframing is an excellent way to handle questions and objections. For example, the price of a product or service is in itself meaningless – it is the audience's perception of it being cheap, expensive or good value that is important. Reframing allows you to change that subjective meaning in order to create the right outcome for your presentation.

10.19   Presentation Aids

10.19.1   Environment

How can you use the physical environment to help you achieve your outcome? You might think about the location of chairs, tables, refreshment, signs, posters – anything that will support you and help you to achieve your outcome.

In Derren Brown's 'Mind Control' TV series, he gets some creative designers to come up with an idea for a brand. Of course, the branding, images and logos were very similar to what he had already drawn and sealed in an envelope, but how? He had carefully planned their journey from their office to his, with posters, stickers, logos on children's sweatshirts, items in shop windows and parcels carried by couriers to influence their thoughts. How could you do the same in your presentation?

10.19.2   Visual Aids

You've probably seen a presentation where the presenter read out the words on the screen verbatim, and you probably thought, "I could read that myself…"

The more words you put on the screen, the less the audience will pay attention to you. When you put words on a slide, the first thing the audience will do is read the words. While they're doing that, they're not listening to you.

If you want to include a presentation script or detailed notes, put them into notes pages, not the main slides. Think of slides as signposts rather than guidebooks and you'll be on the right track.

What other presentation aids can you use to enhance the overall experience?

10.19.3   Computer Projected Slides

Easy and quick to create, easy to share a common layout or style, easy to change when you find out new information five minutes before your presentation!

10.19.4   Whiteboards

Good for keeping track of meetings or informal 'chalk and talk' sessions, not so good for presentations as you have to turn your back to the audience to use them, and you can't prepare your presentation beforehand.

10.19.5   Flipcharts

Good for presentations as you can write them beforehand, use different colours, draw pictures etc, and you can face the audience while using it. Not as easy to change or update as whiteboards.

10.19.6   Music

Very effective for managing your audience's state. Don't underestimate its power.

10.19.7   Anything!

You can use anything to highlight or add some extra dimension to your presentation. The obvious example is product samples or models, but you can use anything you want to give your presentation some extra impact.

Overall, the more ways you can communicate with the audience, the more memorable your presentation will be.

10.20   Tuning in to the Audience

10.20.1   Sensory Language

You can use language which engages different senses to create a richer experience for your learners.

Visual	See	Vision	Sharp
	Picture	Outlook	Background
	Look	Bright	Shine
	Watch	Clear	Reflect
	Perspective	Focus	Eye catching
Auditory	Listen	Quiet	Whistle
	Hear	Amplify	Whine
	Sound	Tell	Roar
	Noise	Resonate	Silent
	Loud	Hum	Tone
Kinaesthetic	Feel	Push	Down
	Touch	Embrace	Ache
	Grab	Warm	Gut reaction
	Hold	Cold	Queasy
	Contact	Sinking	Shaky

Please remember though, there is absolutely no evidence for 'learning styles' or even 'sensory preferences', they simply do not exist. Don't fall into the trap of labelling your learners, instead think about communicating with all of their senses.

10.20.2   Motivation

Some people are motivated towards outcomes, others away from drawbacks. Towards people will be motivated by benefits and will tend to rush into decisions without weighing up the consequences. Away from people will be motivated by savings or avoidance and will tend hold back because of potential problems.

10.20.3   Reference

Some people make decisions based on internal information, others on external information. Internal people use their own experience and tend to think this applies to everyone. External people rely on other people or sources of information.

10.20.4   Choice

Some people need options, others need processes. Options people need alternatives and will create their own if they feel restricted. They often do things in a seemingly random order. Process people need step by step procedures and need to do things in the right order.

Everyone has a preference, and this can be influenced by context and state. Whilst you can quickly profile the people in your audience, the safest approach is to make sure you cover all preferences.

Make a decision because it achieves x and avoids y. You already know that you need to do this because everyone is doing it. By doing this the right way, you're giving yourself more choice.

10.21   Personal Tuning

10.21.1   Congruence

Congruence between your words, movements and words could be the most important aspect of presenting with impact. Similarly, incongruence can be a useful technique worth practising.

10.21.2   Voice

You can have a much greater degree of control over your voice than you might have imagined – not just the volume but also the location in your body where your voice resonates. You can practice moving your voice around your body and listening to the difference it makes. When you are well balanced and breathing properly, your voice will be at its most resonant and compelling.

10.21.3   Balance

It's important to be well balanced, with your centre of gravity well centred. Not only does this mean you can move fluidly, it gives an impression of great presence.

10.21.4   Stage Presence

What is stage presence? Presenting like you mean it, owning the space, voice, posture, gestures are all part of it.

You know how to model strategies, so find someone who you respect as a presenter and learn what they do.

Stage presence is simply a state, and you already know many ways to access useful states. It's useful to set up anchors for useful states so that you can access them easily during your presentation.

Here are some ideas for anchors you can use:

- A big red mental 'On button' (an off button too!)

- A word

- A physical movement

- A piece of music

- An item of clothing

Having said that, I personally do not advocate the use of anchors as resources. States like confidence are not the result of 'getting into' a state, I believe that they are natural states, and all you have to do is stop the things that prevent or take away that natural confidence.

What are the things that affect your confidence, and how can you prevent them?

The kinds of physical anchors that I've given examples of can still be useful in reminding you of certain things, such as timing, your overall feeling of control or just to relax and enjoy yourself.

10.21.5   Posture

Different postures will convey meaning to the audience. It's worth spending some time paying attention to your posture when you present and to develop a comfortably relaxed, open posture when that is helpful to you in your presentation.

10.21.6   Rhythm

Rhythm is one of the key factors in a hypnotic trance induction and is therefore a powerful aspect of any communication.

10.22   Anchoring the Audience

If you read books on NLP-based presentation skills, you will learn that in the first few minutes of your presentation, you can set out anchors that you will use later on. You might want to set anchors for:

- Agreement

- Disagreement

- Reliable companies/You

- Unreliable companies/Your competitors

What else?

You can also set anchors with colours, sounds, music, gestures etc.

You can also practice setting these anchors with the sequence of states you worked out earlier.

Spatial anchoring is, in my opinion, an example of where NLP trainers have jumped on a good idea and in doing so have reduced its effectiveness. If you have seen a trainer who advocates 'spatial anchoring' then you'll possibly have seen a rather deliberate and stilted wandering about on stage, where the speaker's position is supposed to trigger certain states in the audience. As the presentation reaches its climax, they're running backwards and forwards through the different 'anchors'. Personally, I find this exceptionally irritating, which prevents it from working.

I'll go a step further – do not use spatial anchoring, because there is no such thing as spatial anchoring. It is a ludicrous waste of valuable time that you could be using for something more valuable, such as paying attention to your audience instead of planning for where you're going to stand next. At best, all you're influencing is your own state.

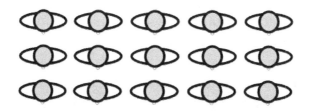

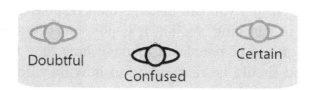

Doubtful   Confused   Certain

I don't know, maybe it works beautifully and I'm just cynical. Maybe most of the people in the audience are thinking, "Why won't he stand still?". Who knows.

Personally, spatial anchoring is not something that I ever consider for my training. It's simply too much hard work, too unreliable, and if you really want to anchor states, there are much neater ways to do it.

If you've trained with me then you will know that anchoring is simply unreliable for an audience because you need to control the timing of the audience's responses. Even self help gurus who supposedly control the state of thousands of people in a football stadium are not really using anchoring, they're getting responses from a few people and then using the phenomenon of social pressure to pull everyone else in.

Anchoring relies on precise timing of the anchor with an existing anchor which leads to a response. Why bother installing a new anchor? Why not just replay the existing anchor? The easiest way to do this is through language, so if your group is small enough, get to know the words that they associate with certain states. We've known that timing was the key for almost 100 years, first as 'Hebbian theory' and more recently as 'Spike Timing Dependent Plasticity', in which the neurons in your brain spontaneously connect with each other based on proximity and timing. You can find out more about this in The NLP Master Practitioner Manual.

The point is that anchoring is something that you do with one person so that you can manage their responses during a technique or coaching session. It is not something that you do with a group of people to manage how they feel. As a trainer, you should be responding to how they do feel, not trying to control them so that they feel how you want them to feel.

Personally, I don't anchor states for my learners. I just present the best training that I can and trust them to manage their own states. I take breaks, I encourage them to have lots to drink and I don't run long days. In my experience, these are all far more important, and controllable, than dancing around on the stage, believing that you're having any impact on the audience's state.

Sometimes, an individual learner will drag down the mood in the whole room. They might be having a breakdown, they might be pushing a particular agenda, who knows. Well, the point is that if you've understood and applied everything you've learned so far, you'll know, and so will your other learners. The best thing you can do is to take a break, because if the learner has their own hidden agenda, no amount of reasoning or clever language will get you out of the hole that you dig for yourself by engaging with them.

The famous physicist Richard Feynman used the phrase 'Cargo Cult Science'. In one of his lectures, he said that South Sea islanders watched aircraft land during the war, bringing food and supplies. After the war, the planes stopped coming. The islanders wanted the planes to return, so they reproduced the conditions for that to happen. They built runways and lit fires along them. They built bamboo control towers and someone would sit in there with coconut shells on his head like earphones. They waited, and the planes didn't come back.

This is what happens when people who don't take the trouble to understand the underlying principles of NLP try to emulate the observable surface features of the techniques. They can't get the same results, so they say that NLP doesn't work. It's like saying that airports don't work, because when you build one, the planes don't come.

When you understand how this all works, and you understand that timing and consistency are vital for anchoring, and you understand what a swish is and how it works, you can easily understand how to elicit states in the audience and how to move them from one state to another.

You don't need any fancy tricks, you don't need spatial anchoring, you just need to focus on setting and maintaining clear rules, delivering the best training that you can, and actually paying attention to what your learners are doing.

You also need to bear in mind the approach that a movie director takes. Think about a film that you've seen recently – it's not all 'action' or 'emotion', is it? The director leads you on a journey, which we will explore later on. The director can't control who goes to the cinema and who likes the film, but if the right people are engaged, they will probably feel a similar range and sequence of emotions. That's a far more useful thing to aim for.

10.23   Getting Attention

Good presenters are very good at getting and keeping the audience's attention. Aside from anchoring, what other techniques can you use? One of the most important is the pattern interrupt.

There's a simple technique you can use at the start of your presentation to reset expectations, which is very useful if you are presenting after your competitors, or if you want to reset the audience's expectations about your subject matter.

For this, you can use a flipchart, whiteboard or even a PC projector is you prepare carefully beforehand.

The technique is a version of the Swish pattern which is something covered on the NLP Practitioner course.

Begin by pacing the audience's expectations, honestly, on the flipchart, concentrating on those that are not useful and that you would like to change. When you have created rapport, tear off the sheet leaving the blank sheet underneath, screw the sheet into a ball and throw it into the corner of the room. Now begin writing what you want the audience's expectations to be.

Actually, there's a step before that: tear the edges of the flipchart sheet along its perforation by about 2 inches or 5 cm so that it tears smoothly when you pull it.

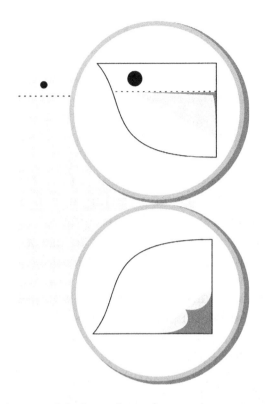

If you're using a whiteboard, make sure you can wipe away quickly and easily. If you're using a PC, make sure your first slide has the audience's real expectations and make the slide after either blank or with the expectations you want.

The swish with the flipchart incorporates a pattern interrupt and therefore relies very much on your ability to lead the audience in order to control the timing.

10.24   Pacing and Leading

Using the state planning approach we covered earlier on, you can lead the audience through a smooth transition of states. The first step is to pace their current state and to then have a clear direction that you want to go in. In order to pace and lead effectively, you must have a clear outcome.

10.25   Direction and Misdirection

Directing the audience's attention can be as simple as saying, "pay attention, because this is very important" so you direct them to remember the parts of your presentation that you want them to.

Misdirection is harder and needs more practice, because you are focussing on what you want the audience to not focus on. Incongruence can be a difficult thing to master but once you have, you will find many ways to use it effectively in your presentations and other communications.

An easy way to misdirect the audience is to use a visual aid. Traditional thinking on presentations is that it is not a good idea to have a lot of text on slides because the audience will stop and read the slide before they carry on listening to you. Of course, while they are not listening, your words are still going in through their ears. You might be able to think of some interesting applications for this idea.

10.26   Questions and Objections

Questions and objections are a wonderful source of feedback for you - they tell you that people are paying attention!

Questions demand a direct answer. Objections often provoke argument. Whilst they may be phrased differently, as the presenter it is not immediately obvious which is which.

Unfortunately, people ask questions for lots of different reasons, only some of which require a direct answer, so it's not always useful for you to answer questions. Here are some possible reasons for asking a question:

- To demonstrate knowledge

- To demonstrate superiority over the presenter

- To disguise an objection

- To get a response from the presenter

- To get a response from another audience member

- To demonstrate attentiveness

- To waste time

- To set up for an attack

- To hide the fact that they weren't listening

- To gain control of the presentation

- To learn something

- To clarify a point they don't understand

If you want to learn more about the motivation behind questions, listen to the political interviews conducted on BBC Radio 4's Today program, every weekday morning. You can listen on the BBC website if you are outside the UK, or I'm sure other countries have similar current affairs programs where ill-tempered interviewers try to get straight answers out of politicians.

The interviewers are masters at asking direct, attacking questions, which practised interviewees are adept at deflecting, whilst sneaking indirect questions past the interviewee's defences. In relation to NLP, they are very good at creating double binds, where either any answer or no answer at all will reveal the truth.

For example, in this recent (paraphrased) exchange, the journalist wanted to know if a Conservative politician had been part of the plot to overthrow Iain Duncan Smith.

Journalist: Is it important for a government to be accountable?

Politician: Absolutely, yes

Journalist: So will you be accountable for demanding his resignation?

Politician: That's a private matter

The journalist's question was a blatant set-up, and the politician's answer is essentially, "yes I did". This wasn't a particularly elegant set-up, but it still trapped an unwary interview subject. I've seen many presenters trapped in exactly the same way.

The solution to this is very simple. You have to repeat the question back, exactly as you heard it. This gives the questioner an opportunity to rephrase their question, and it gives you time to think. From a purely professional point of view, it also means that everyone has heard the question which you're now answering. Anyone sitting behind the questioner is unlikely to have heard it the first time. When you're sure you understand the question, you can then figure out how you want to answer it, presuming that you do actually want to answer it.

10.27   Err...

What do you think might be a word that most presenters will say most often while they're presenting, especially when they're answering a question? Well it's not a word as such, but we'll pretend that it is.

The word is, "Err...."

Let's make ERR a mnemonic. It's a bit of a squeeze but we'll do our best.

Someone asks you a question.

You say, "Err..."

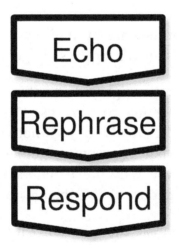

Remember that ERR means that you:

Echo back their question, then

Rephrase it to show you understand, then

Respond if appropriate.

Why is this important? Why not just answer the question?

Firstly, it is genuinely useful to make sure you're answering the question you think you're answering, so you can check this by Echoing it back. When you Echo back the question, the questioner can decide if that's what they really meant to ask you. Also, as I mentioned before, this makes sure that everyone in the audience hears the question that you're about to respond to.

When you **Echo** the question, use the questioner's words exactly. You'll know that pacing their question also builds rapport, reducing the potential for misunderstanding or animosity. Although, personally, I just think it's respectful. I don't bother with rapport-building, I think it's unnecessary.

Secondly, when you **Rephrase** the question, you give the questioner another chance to check that what you understand is what they meant. It also gives you a chance to check that the questioner's motives are genuine.

For example, someone might ask, "Is this analysis reliable?" Of course, you're going to say yes. Why would anyone expect you to say, "Actually, no, it's not very reliable but I was in a hurry to put my report together". What are they really saying? Maybe they don't understand the data and they're hoping that you will give them some more clues.

So you might Rephrase the question with, "Are you asking for statistical reliability data, or would you find case studies more useful?"

In Rephrasing the question, you have appealed to their need either for reassurance or for raw data from which to draw their own conclusions. If their intention was to trip you up, they are now in a dilemma. They can either pick one of the two legitimate options, or they can admit that what they really meant was something else, which is unlikely.

Finally, you can **Respond**, but only if you want to. You may choose to defer the question until later, if it breaks the flow of your presentation, or you may ask the questioner to ask it again when you get to the Q&A section. During your Q&A section itself, you generally would Reply unless the question led to a group discussion and you felt it wasn't necessary to join in. This would usually be the case when the questioner's colleagues do a better job of answering than you could have done yourself!

There are many ways to Respond to a question, and answering it yourself is only one option. You could just as easily reflect the question back to the questioner, or invite other learners to answer. As a trainer, you can use anything that happens as a learning opportunity.

It's inevitable during NLP Practitioner training that students will ask for help with a personal issue. Maybe they want help to give up smoking or make some other personal changes. My answer is always, "Yes, if we can do it with the group so that everyone can learn from the experience." If they say no, and it isn't a genuinely personal issue, the chances are that just want my personal attention.

10.28   When to Take Questions?

Taking questions is an important consideration for both presenters and trainers. As a presenter, you have an obvious block of time which you may or may not prefer to have interrupted. As a trainer, you might be giving demonstrations or explaining something that you want to complete, and you want to control whether your learners can ask questions or wait until the end of that segment.

Having previously said that I don't use spatial anchoring, I've realised that there is one thing that I do which is similar, but I wouldn't call it anchoring exactly. I typically have four positions in a training room which I use to control the interactivity in the room. They are:

- Standing at the front

- Standing to the side

- Sitting at the front

- Sitting at the back

You can probably work out what these positions signal to the audience, and it's really quite obvious. It's more to do with ownership of the space than anchoring, though my learners generally get used to seeing me in these positions and responding accordingly.

If you really can't be bothered to work it out, and assuming that you have already put yourself in an imaginary audience and watched me moving between those four positions, and you still can't figure it out, here are some clues.

Standing at the front	I'm in charge and I'm talking
Standing to the side	I'm in charge, you can talk
Sitting at the front	Open forum
Sitting at the back	Someone else is in charge

Note that this is not spatial anchoring, because I don't believe in spatial anchoring.

Or is it?

Maybe what I'm doing is replaying existing anchors that call to mind experiences from school and work?

When I move to the side, I literally 'get out of the way', and when I'm standing, I'm in an implied position of authority over the audience. When I sit down, I put myself on the audience's level, which encourages interactivity. As soon as I stand up again, their eyes are back on me and I'm setting the pace again. If one of the students is presenting, perhaps as part of an exercise, I sit at the back so that they have the presentation space completely at their command.

I find this to be a very simple and effective 'flow control' mechanism.

Whether you're going to take questions throughout the presentation or at the end, you need to do these things:

- Allow time in your schedule – as a rule of thumb, plan your presentation to last about three-quarters of your allocated time.

- Handle questions using the ERR format, otherwise you will get sidetracked

- Preferably have someone else manage the Q&A

- Make a note of the questions so that you can incorporate your answers into your presentation

Whether you take questions in the middle or at the end, you handle them in the same way, otherwise you hand control of the presentation back to the audience, and that is a very bad thing.

What most presenters do is announce that their presentation has ended when they have run out of things to talk about, then invite questions.

Invitation setup	Room setup	Presentation	Close	Q&A

Wrong!

What we actually need to do is this:

Invitation setup	Room setup	Presentation	Q&A	Close

Do you see the difference?

- You hand control of the room back to the audience only when you have finished

- You dictate the pace of the questions

- You decide when there are no more questions

- You decide when the presentation ends

- You have the golden opportunity to incorporate the questions into your summary

If you close the presentation and then invite questions, you are telling the audience that you failed to cover everything they needed. Their perception will be that they got what they needed by asking you questions. The presentation fizzles out when there are no more questions.

If you invite questions and then close the presentation, you are telling the audience that you are flexible and authoritative, and that you are adapting to their needs. Their perception will be that the presentation was interactive and that it gave them everything they needed. The presentation ends cleanly when you close it.

Compare it to a film. Does a film end, or does it just fizzle out when the characters have nothing left to say?

When you have a number of people presenting and you have a panel Q&A session at the end, the approach is a little different.

In this situation, one person will have the role of managing the questions. Here's what they do:

1. Invite questions from the audience

2. Select someone to ask a question

3. Repeat the question so that the whole audience can hear it, and clarifies it if necessary

4. Asks which speaker will respond, or selects one if the choice is clear

5. Checks that the answer is satisfactory

6. Moves to the next question or closes the Q&A

You can see how steps 3 and 4 are partly designed to give the speaker time to think of a good answer! When you're presenting by yourself, pausing and clarifying (ERR) gives you valuable time to think.

10.29   Feedback

How do you know you are on the right track? What signs do you pay attention to that let you know if your presentation is having the right effect on the audience, or if there is anything you need to change?

Could you suggest a feedback mechanism to the audience at the start of your presentation? Could you even build in an unconscious feedback mechanism?

How can you manage the audience's state in order to control feedback or interactivity?

One thing I've seen people do at the end of a presentation is ask for feedback. Think back to outcomes and you'll realise that this is very dangerous. If the audience didn't know you were going to ask for feedback then what they give you will be random and reactive at best. This is one reason why the feedback forms they give out at the end of training courses are so useless. The audience are paying attention for the purpose of learning something, not for the purpose of evaluating the training. Completely different!

If you are going to ask for feedback, make sure you say so at the start so that the audience know to pay attention and you consequently get the kind of feedback that is useful to you.

10.30   Closing

It's very important that you give yourself time to close the presentation properly. Here are some points to bear in mind:

1. Remind the audience of the purpose of your presentation

2. Remind the audience of the key points

3. Remind the audience of the questions that you answered

4. Ask the audience to do what you want them to do

5. Tell the audience what they need to do right now

6. Make sure the audience knows how to get in touch with you

7. And always remember to say thank you!

It's a good idea to future pace at the end of your presentation, and summarising the presentation itself is the ideal foundation because you create a momentum by starting in the past and then moving forwards in time.

By summarising what you have already covered in your presentation, the audience will shift into an agreement state that makes it easier for them to agree with your suggestions for future plans or next steps.

For example, "So you've heard all about presenting, and I've told you about some of the applications of NLP in presenting, and as you have read through this, you may have thought of some questions, and as this chapter begins to draw to a close you might think of more ways to put this into practice, tomorrow, next week, next month and as you use these techniques with every presentation you deliver, you can find yourself becoming more and more effective and elegant with each new experience".

10.31   Your Identity as a Presenter

The logical levels model is a nice integration tool which helps you to increase alignment between your identity (how you see yourself), your behaviour and your environment.

An exercise like this gets the person to create a new identity which encompasses and embraces their new abilities and provides the foundation for creating new behaviour in new situations. By integrating skills in this way, the person will automatically become a more flexible, more effective presenter, even in situations you have never covered during the training course.

10.31.1.1   Logical Levels

Set out 5 spaces on the floor to represent 5 logical levels. You can mark them with pieces of paper if you like.

Step onto Environment. What is the environment for you as a presenter? The location, the audience, other factors.

Step onto Behaviour. What do you see yourself doing as a great presenter?

Step onto Capabilities. What skills have you developed?

Step onto Beliefs. What is now true for you as a presenter? What do you believe about yourself? What do you believe about your audiences?

Step onto Identity. What kind of presenter have you become?

Walk back though each level, taking with you what you have learned about yourself at each level.

10.32   Timeline

Where a logical levels exercise integrates through a person's mental hierarchy, a timeline creates an experience and connects new skills which will continue to develop and grow over time, integrating through past, present and future.

10.32.1.1   Timeline

Imagine looking into the future and seeing a number of presentations that lie ahead of you, becoming more ambitious and important as time goes on. Take a step into that future, stepping into the next presentation you'll be doing. Be aware of the sense of satisfaction at presenting with impact, and see some of the new behaviours you exhibit. Take another step into the next presentation and see how you have developed again, noticing how that feels.

Continue to step forward through future presentations, being aware of how you grow and develop with each one. When you have arrived at a point in the future that you are comfortable with, stop and ask yourself, "what kind of presenter have I become?"

Now, turn and look back and see how much you have developed since you began. Walk back to the present moment, taking with you the new experiences and resources. When you arrive back at the present, turn and face the future once more. Imagine the future looking bigger and brighter now and being much closer than you had imagined. Take a moment to enjoy the future that awaits you.

A timeline is especially important for people who were nervous of presenting. A common concern is, "I feel good now, but I know that as soon as I go back to work and have to present for real, I'll be nervous again". By now, you'll recognise this as a worry program, where the person imagines something will happen in the future and then makes it happen through their responses in the present.

10.33   Bringing Your Ideas To Life

I think that the ability to present is probably the most important professional skill that you can master. Regardless of how good your ideas are, if you cannot communicate them to a large number of people in an inspiring and compelling way, they will never reach their full potential.

Every year, the number of new patents registered increases and yet this still represents the tip of the iceberg. As many as 99% of new ideas just gather dust and never become reality. People will infer the importance of your idea, not from the content but from the way you communicate it.

I find that successful executives very quickly learn a survival mechanism which protects them from the overwhelming demands on their time – they say no to everything. They do not have the knowledge or experience necessary to evaluate every idea on its own merits, so they learn to judge the importance of an idea from the persistence and passion of the person presenting the idea.

Whether you are creating global businesses or inspiring children, the art of public speaking will always be key to the way we relate to each other as a species. After putting into practice the ideas in this chapter, you will have a much better chance of making your ideas, beliefs and desires a reality.

11 The Art of Performance

If you ever sat at your desk in school, listening to a teacher droning on and on, listing facts for you to copy down in your book then you know that the transmission of knowledge alone does not constitute training.

At Practitioner level, the syllabus defines what you'll train but not how you'll train it. At Master Practitioner, the syllabus is more about developing skills, and in my Master Practitioner training, I focus on the use of those skills in modelling which is, after all, the origin of NLP.

If you don't think about how you will deliver that knowledge and those skills then you are very likely to deliver your training in the image of how you were trained.

For many trainers who trained with Bandler, that means sitting on a stool at the front of the room, telling stories for hour after hour and pretending that your students are 'learning unconsciously'. Well, they might be unconscious but that doesn't mean they're learning. NLP is a practical art, it involves techniques which were originally created by Bandler and Grinder, and allegedly a few other people. How can you learn to do something by listening to someone tell amazing stories about times when they did it? If I tell you about the time I swam the English Channel, will you learn how to swim? I didn't even do that, by the way. However I'm sure all the amazing stories from NLP trainers aren't made up at all. Or embellished in any way.

Some people are shocked, even offended by my disrespect for the training methods employed by notable NLP trainers, but I draw your attention to the 40 years of peer-reviewed academic research on the subjects of neuroscience, psychology and learning that has taken place since NLP was created. For NLP to be a progressive and seriously-regarded discipline, we must be prepared to question and challenge accepted truths. If we can't, won't or don't do that then NLP does indeed become a cult, and I don't think any of us like the idea of that. So my disrespect is actually a thirst for innovation and excellence, and to achieve that, we must be prepared to forget everything that we know. The creators and contributors to NLP have all done a marvellous job, yet remember their own words, that "the positive worth of an individual is held constant, while the value of the internal and/or external behaviour is questioned". In other words, I have great respect for them and their work, and total disrespect for a body of knowledge which is not peer-reviewed, tested and updated. However, the contributors to the body of knowledge are not the problem, because they are all working hard to further our understanding of the human condition. The problem is that their knowledge and their latest developments get lost inside the system, and the people who are training Practitioners today are often repeating what they've been taught instead of thinking for themselves.

If we're going to model an expert, we have to take their background and environment into account. Allegedly, Bandler started chain smoking when he modelled Erickson, because Erickson smoked and so that might be important. We don't know *why* Erickson smoked. So because Bandler sits on a stool and tells stories, are you going to do the same? And because I like making silly jokes, are you going to do the same? You've got to work out what's right for you. Your trainer may have sat on a stool because he couldn't manage anything more physically demanding. Who knows?

However cleverly you structure your stories with hypnotic commands and nested loops to create rich imaginary experiences for the listener, the simple fact is that they are not having a primary sensory experience and therefore this style of training falls squarely in the category of 'cognitive learning', and we've already seen the limitations of that style.

Maybe you think that by telling stories, you are instilling the beliefs and attitudes necessary for NLP to work. If we say that our students only need to perform the techniques and trust the techniques to work, then we are working in the category of 'behavioural learning', so certainly some change in the decision making processes behind those behaviours is valuable. However, I would argue that the most efficient way to change those decision processes is through contrasting first hand experiences. "Here's a technique where you don't observe the client, and here's one where you do. What's the difference?", for example.

Our sensory receptors detect difference, therefore difference becomes information, information becomes knowledge, knowledge becomes behaviour. If we take a short cut and just jump straight to the knowledge then the only raw data that you're giving your student is "because I said so", and I'm sure you've had experience of that, maybe as a teenager or when working for an oppressive boss. If the student doesn't know *why* they're doing a certain thing then you have achieved behavioural learning, at best.

Maybe stories provide a context for learning? Perhaps they convey experiences which the students have not yet had so that the students can develop greater confidence? Even in that case, confidence is not something that you can give another person, you can only show that you have confidence in them. Therefore, letting them practice techniques on each other is your primary way of showing confidence that they're not going to break each other.

Overall, what we're looking for is a way for you to add value to the raw experience of the learner, so that there is a tangible benefit for them in attending your training instead of reading a book or simply figuring it out for themselves.

I'm sure you've sat through a presentation or training session where the trainer simply stood and read out the words that you could see projected onto the screen. You probably wondered what value they were adding. Perhaps if you asked any questions, they said, "I'll take that away and get an answer for you".

You probably felt that the training session was a waste of your time.

What value did the trainer add to the notes and slides? What was added by having a human present the material rather than just emailing the notes for everyone to read in their own time?

Information needs a transmitter and a receiver in order to get it from one place to another. Is that all there is to it? Clearly not, otherwise every trainer and presenter would be the same, only the information would change. That is definitely not the case.

Information in itself is not useful, it is only useful in context, and that context creates meaning.

"What did you think of my presentation?"

"Three"

"Three what? Three out of ten? Three out of five?"

"Three apples"

"Eh?"

One of the earliest things that your brain, specifically your visual cortex, does, is to figure out the difference between what you're interested in, and what's behind it. You learn to distinguish between 'object' and 'field'. This creates a unique relationship between the two which defines how we interact with the object. Your ability to make this distinction is quite remarkable, as I will now demonstrate.

Here is a pattern of dots:

If I take some of those dots and move them, just a tiny amount, you might see a pattern:

This demonstration shows how your brain is able to detect patterns, and also irregularities in those patterns, and how those irregularities create meaning.

As a trainer, you transmit information to your learners. The way in which your transmission differs from mine or any other trainer's defines your performance, and your performance shapes the audience's experience.

As a NLP Trainer, you need to know the syllabus and techniques of NLP, inside out. You must be able to demonstrate the techniques and get a 'result' first time, every time. You must not get sidetracked by your demonstration subject's issue, because you are not delivering a coaching session, you are delivering a training demonstration.

You must also have a solid training plan so that you consistently deliver exactly what you planned for each day of training. If every technique runs over by 20 minutes, you'll have lost a day by the end of your course and you'll either rush to cram in the last few techniques, or worse, you'll skip techniques altogether so that your students are no longer getting the training that they paid for.

Once you have those two elements, you have to work on your performance, because that is how you will define yourself as a trainer, and that is why your students will recommend you to their friends.

Consider that the same applies when you're coaching. Using Meta Model, you will know the client's issue before they think they've told you. At what point do you reveal that knowledge? Do you 'cut to the chase' in the first two minutes and effect your custom intervention? If you did, how might your client feel?

Think of an actor who you admire. What is it that sets her or him apart? Could it partly be in their natural, believable delivery? The irony is that the actor knows the lines ahead of time, yet their reactions are as if the conversation is unfolding before your eyes. It's as if they forget that they know what's coming, even though they do.

The TV 'mentalist' Derren Brown gave a beautiful demonstration of this in the card trick 'Extreme Mental Effort' on his Devil's Picturebook video. The trick is technically simple. In fact, it's so simple that you would be amazed at how he does it, and on my training courses, no-one has ever guessed it, because his performance is so convincing. In the following discussion with his colleague, Derren reveals that he knew the chosen card from the beginning but has to forget that he knows it in order for his performance to be genuine.

When you're performing a demonstration, you have to do the same. Let's say you demonstrate a swish. The client will be different, and their issue will be different each time, yet when you know the swish and you're confident in your delivery, the swish will actually be the same each time. Of course, your students won't know that, because they'll only see the demonstration once.

How could the swish be the same each time when each client is unique and special? Yes, they're very special. And yet, they are the same. Stimulus, response, undesired outcome. The names and places will change, the process will always be the same – because you are demonstrating a swish, and therefore you will be asking for someone to help you who has an issue which exactly fits the technique you want to demonstrate.

When I run Practitioner or Master Practitioner training, I know that my demonstrations will look good. For a start, if you can't master a technique yourself, how can you confidently demonstrate it?

On top of that, if you make your demo convoluted and complicated, how are your students going to feel about trying out the technique for themselves?

Therefore, making your demonstrations look good is not about you showing what an awesome trainer you are, it's about giving your students confidence. When they see your demonstrations work first time, every time, they will think, "That looks easy, I can do that!" and will enter the practice sessions more confidently.

They may then find that the technique does or does not turn out how they expected, so you have to remember what is important:

1. They had a go

2. They noticed what happened

When you perform your demonstration, just stick to the technique. Don't be clever, don't show off, don't improvise. Do perform the technique as if you're a Practitioner yourself, do focus on the basic technique, do stick to the script.

If you think you're performing a coaching session with your demo subject, you'll wander off the technique in order to get a 'result' with the subject. Your students will be totally confused about what you're asking them to do and then you'll have to explain what you did and what they don't need to worry about because that was just for the demo subject, not part of the technique. Their heads will be spinning, they won't have a clear idea in mind for what they need to practice, their techniques won't work effectively, they won't be able to use the techniques as a result and they'll be left with an unsatisfying impression of NLP and of you. Do you want that? Of course not. So pay attention. You're not running a coaching session, you're giving a technique demo. Stick to the demo. Oh, but what if the demo doesn't work? Won't that make you look bad? Come on, think straight. You must know by now that you have to be clear about what you mean by 'work'. Does the technique get a desirable result for the demo subject? Irrelevant! Who cares? They're there to learn, not to get therapy. Forget them. You could be using a shop dummy for all it matters. The only advantage to using a live subject is that their responses show the students what to expect.

'Work' means that your students know what to do. So a demo that 'works' is a demo that clearly shows your students how to perform the technique. But what if their 'client' doesn't respond in the way you expect? Irrelevant. Let the technique do its job. If your students don't get the result they expect, that's a problem with their expectations. They should be paying attention to their client, not looking for the responses that they expect. Any questions will be addressed in the feedback session after the practice.

Each NLP technique is very simple. Very, very simple. Each one has a very clear script for what you need to do, so the first thing you have to do is learn the techniques. For you to have gotten this far in your training, you must be very confident with the techniques already but you never know, you might have had a poor trainer before now. I've met Practitioners who didn't know the swish, and I've met a Trainer who had never heard of the presuppositions of NLP. How the hell? Never mind.

When you know the techniques then you can perform them without having to look at your notes. That will inspire confidence in your students. If you know what you're doing then it must be easy to learn.

Next, you have to think about where you'll perform your demo. Can your students actually see you? How you stand to make the technique easy for you is not necessarily going to make it easy for your students.

Look at these two examples, which do you think will make it easier for your students to follow what you're doing?

As you are performing your demo, give a running commentary on what you're doing and, most importantly, how you know when to do it. While the techniques are very explicit, they don't tell you when to offer the outcome or how to know when the client is sufficiently dissociated, for example. Your commentary needs to describe what you're looking for, what you're seeing and what decisions you're making as a result of that.

During the subsequent feedback session, question your students and help them to reflect on their experiences so that they can figure out the reasons for what happened. If they feel that they encountered problems, help them to come up with ideas for what to do differently. If you think it's necessary, get them to try the technique again using some of their ideas.

As I said, getting a result for the client is irrelevant because the person you're working with isn't a client, they're a demo subject.

If you were seeing a real client for a real coaching session, would you start by saying, "I'm going to do a swish, now think of something you have a strong reaction to that you'd like to change". The client might reply, "Erm, actually I was looking for help with my diet. I don't really have a strong reaction to salad, I just prefer cake."

Of course not. You'd start by asking them what they want. However, if you do that during your training, you'll be drawn into therapy and the course won't follow a consistent structure. So we need to cover the required techniques in a logical order and at the same time give our students an experience of change. How can we achieve this?

The answer, as always, is very simple. You don't just ask for any old volunteer to help you with a demo, you ask for someone who has a specific issue in mind which fits the technique you want to demonstrate. Then, guess what? The demo produces an impressive result for your subject and the other students are amazed. More importantly, your other students see that the technique is effective, which gives them confidence to have a go. When they see that the technique 'works', because their focus is on the application of the technique, they know that they can trust the technique to do what you say it will do.

I was once running a workshop at a NLP practice group and I said something about choosing people who are responsive for demonstrations. Someone asked, "How do you know who will be responsive?"

The answer is, of course, that you ask a question and see who answers it. To make life easier, it helps if you can ask the *right* question.

When you start talking about a particular technique, you'll create a frame of reference within which your students will place themselves. If you talk about phobias, or undesirable reactions, or dilemmas, or a person at work who really irritates you, the students will make sense of this (convert to raw sensory data) through their own experiences. As soon as you tell your first story, or describe the technique, or ask if your students can share their experiences, they are 'tuned in' to the technique. When you choose your demonstration subject, you have then stacked the odds in your favour. You know that *any* of them would be a good subject!

Contrast this with something that I have seen many times in training:

Trainer: "Can I have someone to help me with a demo?"

Students look at each other nervously.

Eventually a student joins the trainer.

Trainer: "Great! Can you think of a phobia that you have?"

Student: "Erm... not really"

The trainer then digs around for a few minutes until they manage to identify something that they can use in the Fast Phobia Cure, and the results are predictably uninspiring...

Trainer: "So, how do you feel now about your phobia?"

Student: "Erm... OK I guess"

There couldn't be a worse way to demonstrate a powerful technique. It reminds me of a stage hypnosis training course where we put on a public performance at the end. One of the students, who was a car salesman during the day (if that makes any difference) opened his act by asking for "a victim" to join him on the stage. (Cue tumbleweed)

How you set up and describe the technique will make your students *want* to join you for a demo. They will see other students having a powerful experience, and they'll want to share in that. The other students will see something that inspires them to have a go for themselves.

So, you've selected your demonstration subject. They don't know that they've been selected, they think they volunteered. Once they're at the front of the room with you, what do you do with them?

If you search YouTube for the NENLP channel you'll see a video of me at the 2015 NLP Conference, entitled "Everything you know about NLP is wrong". In it, you'll see a couple of technique demonstrations which show you how I do it. However, that is not how you should do it. You need to work out your own style, and that has to be based on your personality.

What I'm trying to tell you is that, whether you think about it or not, you are a performer, and your training is a performance. If you don't think about it seriously and constructively, that performance will be based on:

- Your past experiences of learning

- Your fears

- Your habits

Yet if you do give some thought to your own performance, it will be based on:

- Your best ideas

- Your personal goals

- Your hopes for your students

So that's really it – you're a performer whether you like it or not, so you might as well be the best performer that you can be, which means not trying to emulate someone else's performance. The world already has enough tribute acts, it doesn't need another one, especially when your own personality, experiences and passions are far more interesting and valuable than anything you could learn from anyone else.

Your own experiences are, of course, wonderful and uplifting and inspiring, and also painful, desolate and frightening. The actor Jack Lemmon said, "If you really do want to be an actor who can satisfy himself and his audience, you need to be vulnerable."

But what if you don't believe that you have what it takes to be a great trainer, a great performer? What if you feel that you have no charisma, no gravitas? Maybe you do, maybe you don't, is it important? If you feel that you don't have that special 'something', that's probably because the person who inspired you was different than you are, and you don't know how to be them. Every expert's advice is 'just be yourself', but what if being yourself just isn't very good?

The actor Michael Caine said, "I'm a skilled professional actor. Whether or not I've any talent is beside the point."

It really doesn't matter if you think you're any good or not, what's important is that you practice, you learn from that practice and you connect with people.

Whilst on the subject of what actors said, here's a quote from Meryl Streep; "I'm curious about other people. That's the essence of my acting. I'm interested in what it would be like to be you."

Being a great trainer, a great performer, is much easier when you stop trying to perform and instead, simply connect with your audience. Let them see you. So many trainers of NLP, and self-help in general, portray a chiselled, white-teethed, big-haired image of perfection, and that's just not credible. Maybe if you're with 10,000 people in a stadium then you want a polished performance, but when you're in a smaller, more intimate environment, is that what you want?

At a local practice group in the early 2000s, an up-and-coming NLP trainer, now a big name in the UK, came to present a workshop. He strutted in, his designer shoes clattering on the harsh tiles of the primary school classroom floor. With strong, deliberate movements, he took off his jacket, folded it inside out and laid it on a stool at the front of the room so that the Armani label could be seen by all. He reached up to sweep back his hair, hiding his bald spot and revealing the sparkling Armani belt buckle. Who knows, or cares, if the audience were impressed by this performance? You can decide for yourself what it says about him, and also what it says about me. The point is that none of this was accidental, but whether it was suited to a small local practice group in a school classroom is a different matter. It is who he is, and for that we can applaud his consistency.

Finally, the film actress and founder of an acting school Stella Adler noted that, "The word theatre comes from the Greeks. It means the seeing place. It is the place people come to see the truth about life and the social situation."

I put it to you that this is the reason why people will attend your training. They want to see the truth, in themselves and others, and they want that truth to be good and beautiful. They want to believe that the world is a better place than it seems, that there is hope for themselves and for others, that people sometimes do the wrong things for the right reasons, because not everyone can have everything they want. They want to learn how to make sense of a life that is enlightening yet disheartening, inspiring yet frustrating, thrilling and yet demoralising, a life of contradictions.

In all of this, you are not just a trainer, in fact you are not just a performer. You are a role model. Not for perfection, but for the ongoing process of perfecting, of learning from your mistakes, of overcoming your failures, of rising above what life throws at you and, above all, showing that everything is possible.

11.1.1   Awesome Demonstrations

Here's my checklist for giving awesome demonstrations.

1. Know the techniques, inside out

2. Define the technique in a way which will select the person who will be the best demo subject

3. Ask for a demo subject who has the specific issue that fits the technique you're demonstrating

4. You're not coaching, so stick to the demo, no matter what happens

5. Stand or sit so that your audience can see what you're doing

6. Describe the key points before, during and after your demo in a 'running commentary'

7. Give a time limit for the practice session

8. When the time is up, call everyone back together and ask them what they found, noticed, discovered or experienced

9. Reframe judgements such as "it worked" or "it didn't work" with, "What happened?"

[12] One Step Ahead

I'm sure you've seen NLP trainers talking about sensory acuity, paying attention in great detail to every twitch of the client's eyebrow. This is ridiculous. Focusing on sensory acuity creates a whole lot of work for you, which is all completely unnecessary.

By the time you reach the level of NLP Master Practitioner, you must have stopped responding to your clients, you must have stopped chasing them around and trying to keep up with their every action and reaction. Isn't that what you learned in your Master Practitioner training?

As a Master Practitioner, you are one step ahead of your clients, and as a NLP Trainer, you will be one step ahead of your learners?

How?

Like that. I already knew that your next question would be "How?" You think that you had a free choice, but you didn't. You think that you were in control, but control is an illusion.

You don't need to follow your clients or students, you need to lead them.

Most NLP Trainers teach anchoring as a way of accessing a 'resource state' such as confidence or relaxation. Firstly, confidence is not a state. Secondly, this is such a trivial application of anchoring, and it's a waste of time because, in order to apply an anchor such as a touch on the arm, you first have to elicit an existing anchor. When you ask your student to remember a time when they felt a certain way, you are eliciting anchors. There is really no need to attach other anchors to these, because your student or client has already given you the most versatile anchors that you'll need – words.

Let's consider the example of a NLP Practitioner technique where timing is the most critical aspect – the swish. You simply cannot perform an effective swish if you are responding to the client, because of the signal delay in both your brain and the client's brain.

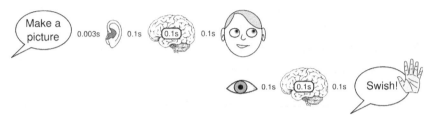

The delays shown in the diagram are the absolute best case signal delay and reaction times. In practice, your client will take around half a second to respond to your instruction, and you'll take about the same time to respond to their reaction. Your sensory acuity is irrelevant, it's the signal delay that causes your incompetence, and it affects all of us.

The only way that you can correctly time the swish is to start moving your hand before you ask your client to picture the 'problem' trigger.

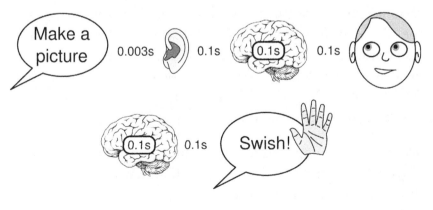

The swish uses a pattern interrupt to disrupt an existing anchor, but if we only interrupt the client, the original program will complete after a moment of confusion. Therefore, we need to introduce a new state, which is triggered by a new anchor, in order to fully distract the client from the 'problem' and introduce change.

If we break the swish down, what we see is a second anchor which triggers a state, part way through a first anchor triggering a state. The first state cannot fully form because the client's attention is grabbed by the swish, and the second state takes over.

Anchoring is therefore a way of controlling the client's responses so that you can control the reprogramming of those responses. If you don't use anchors to control the client, you will always be behind them, trying frantically to catch up, and always being half a second too late. From your point of view, your timing will be spot on, because your brain edits out the delay so that you think your reactions are instantaneous. However, an observer will see the delay.

You can prove this by throwing something to a student without any warning. The student thinks that they react instantly, however the other students will be able to observe the delay. If you then practice throwing and catching, the other students will see the delay reduce as the first student gets used to catching and learns to anticipate the throw. Anticipation through rehearsal is the way that we compensate for a signal delay.

When I was younger and better suited to running around, I played badminton, and one thing that I was very good at was serving. In tennis, a fast server can get the ball moving at 100mph, which is much too fast for the receiving player to follow. The only way to return such a fast serve is by guessing at where the ball might be. Badminton serves are not as violent as they can be in tennis, and the shuttlecock is designed to fly slowly, giving it plenty of time in the area, during which the receiving player can move a good distance across the course. The objective, therefore is to get your opponent off balance so that he or she cannot move to meet the shuttlecock.

I would look in one corner of my opponent's area and wait to see his weight shift. As soon as I saw that, I'd serve to the opposite corner. No matter how good my opponent's reflexes, it was extremely difficult for him to quickly switch direction and get across the court in time to return the serve.

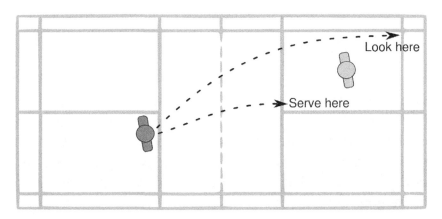

If an opponent 'got wise' to what I was doing, I'd change the corners, serving to my opponent's far backhand, often the very hardest place to reach. In short, don't serve to where your opponent is, serve to where they're not. If they're agile, serve to where they think they're not going to be.

A good player might wait in the centre and not anticipate, but this is no help when the serve is very short, because there often isn't time to see where the shuttlecock is going and reach it before it hits the floor.

If you're a football fan, I'm sure you have spent many hours berating your favourite team's inability to either score or save penalties, where a player has a clear kick at the opponent's goal.

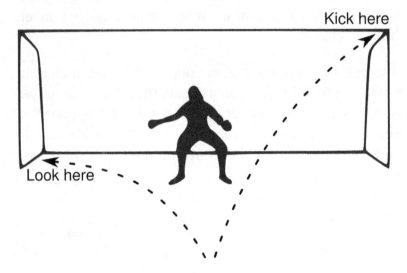

Teams spend time specifically practising penalties. Just like in the badminton example, a player will look into one corner of the goal and start his run up to kick the ball. As he sees the goalkeeper's weight shift in the wrong direction, he switches his own balance and aims for the opposite corner of the goal.

The goal kicker is trying to get one step ahead of the goalkeeper, so goalkeepers who are good at saving penalties don't wait for the kick, they carefully observe the opposing players and learn their patterns. A good goalkeeper is already moving before the kicker has reached the ball. From a spectator's point of view, it looks as if the goalkeeper had very fast reflexes, but this cannot be the case.

Sometimes the kicker 'gets wise' and changes their pattern but, more often than not, they have their favourite penalty target areas in the goal.

Communicating an intention which is different to your actual intention in order to throw an opponent off balance is very much like the skill of 'multi-level communication' which is part of the SNLP certification criteria for Master Practitioner and Trainer, in that you have to get used to balancing two different intentions and acting on them at the same time. Once again, it's so much easier just to keep one step ahead, staying in control of the process that you're following.

As a NLP Trainer, you will come across various learning barriers and strategies. Remembering that every behaviour has a positive intention, every barrier to learning is preceded by an intention to do something useful. For example, a student who doesn't write anything down proves that they are smart, a 'good learner', but they then struggle to remember the steps of an exercise and get frustrated because they don't like feeling stupid.

Feeling stupid was the barrier to learning, but it was the end result of a strategy that the student created in order to prove that they are not stupid.

Therefore, in order to be one step ahead of your learners, you can't respond to their learning barriers once they've hit them. You have to anticipate what those barriers are likely to be, and luckily, they tell you the moment they enter the room, or beforehand, if you've thought carefully about your joining instructions.

Here's an example from a pre-course questionnaire that I send out prior to my courses:

"What do you imagine gaining from the course?"

"A higher understanding of NLP, people, situations, drivers, motivations and the 'opposite forces'."

If you apply Meta Model to that statement, you will see that it is heavily loaded with presuppositions about status and conflict. That one sentence contains everything that you need to know about this student's approach to learning, their preconceptions and the barriers that they will create.

In order to imagine what someone will gain from the course, they have to imagine the process they'll go through in order to gain it, complete with whatever obstacles they have put in their own way. I don't have to figure out what my students' learning barriers are, I already know before they arrive for the first day of training.

By getting to know your learners before the training starts, you will be one step ahead. However, you'll still have to be on your toes, because your learners are facing their demons while learning about NLP, and that can create all kinds of interesting behaviours.

Now, I realise that you may have spent many hours developing your sensory acuity, and that many other NLP trainers have told you that this is very important in order to respond to your clients, and that I am now telling you that sensory acuity is irrelevant, because you're not responding to your clients – you simply can't think that fast.

I realise that this may come as a surprise to you, and that you may at first reject the idea because it seems very important to pay attention to your clients, until you realise the following key points:

1. The laws of physics dictate that you are physically incapable of responding fast enough to effect change

2. You don't want to be where your clients have been, you want to be where they want to be

When you look at it from this point of view, it seems obvious that you can't respond quickly enough to anchor or swish, and if you can't perform those two fundamental building blocks then none of the other techniques will work effectively.

The only chance you've got is to know in advance where your client wants to be, and be there waiting for them, ready to offer them a hand up.

13 Handling Problems

As a trainer, and especially as a NLP Trainer, you will encounter problems. Your training will not run smoothly to plan. Your students will not have the exact experience that you would like them to have. And, particularly with this kind of subject, you will have students reacting in a way which may be disruptive to the group.

The kinds of behaviours which I've seen include:

Distracting behaviours, including excessive joking around, changing the subject, telling long stories, using techniques other than what they are being asked to practise, dominating breaks in order to delay other students from returning to the training.

Attention seeking, including the open discussion of detailed and personal issues and frequent requests for help.

Hiding, ranging from sitting at the back to disappearing completely for long periods of time, perhaps to take 'important' phone calls.

I've had two female colleagues who, on the Practitioner assessment day, disappeared for the entire morning because one of them had a really sensitive issue and needed a longer coaching session. This removed them from observation and denied them and other students a fair assessment.

I've had a student who insisted on single-handedly cooking a complex evening meal which used up ingredients that had been bought for other students and obligated other students to be grateful for all the trouble gone to.

I've had a student who objected to being left out of a private conversation with another student and then pretended to hurt her back in order to get other students to gather round her and soothe her. Her back problem came and went depending on whether she remembered to keep up the pretence.

I've had a student who ignored the instruction about where to go for practice exercises and took her fellow student to her bedroom in order to avoid being observed and to gain an advantage by making the other student feel uncomfortable.

Fundamentally, what these all represent is a student's reaction to fear. In the course of practising NLP techniques, your students will have to work on real issues, and those real issues can bring those underlying fears very much to the surface. We all avoid showing our fears because we don't want to be exploited by others, however our fears are as plain as the noses on our faces, revealed by the very behaviours that we engage in to hide them.

Above all else, remember:

- Your job is to take care of all of your students, not any one student

- Your students are not there for free therapy, so any such work must benefit group learning

- You are a NLP Trainer, set an example accordingly

- Don't stand for any nonsense, reflect these behaviours back as an example of the client's desire to hide their fears, which is completely normal and also temporary

The simplest way to deal with these problems is to prevent them in the way that you open your training, and the way in which you enforce rules throughout. My examples above might sound awful, and actually they are, but they're from almost 20 years of training NLP and compared to other courses I've attended I think that I'm doing OK. Also, on recent courses, students have specifically commented on how amazed they were that the group were so disciplined, especially over timekeeping at breaks. I'll share with you how I achieve that, and then ask you to come up with your own method to create the working environment that's right for you.

What surprises many people is that in all of my training, both NLP and corporate, I don't ask people to turn their phones off. You would think this would lead to more disruption, but it actually leads to less. The key principle is that I am responsible for delivering the best training possible, the students are responsible for being there, paying attention and asking questions if they don't understand. If they're not there, or they want to read messages on their phone, that's fine by me.

I'm sure you've been in a meeting or training course and you phone has buzzed in your pocket. You know it's a message. Is it a reply that you've been waiting for all day? When is the next break due? What can you do? Could you pretend to go to the toilet? Could you sneak a quick look? Sorry, what were you saying?

While your students are worrying about their messages, they're not listening to you. They are present in body but not in spirit. Therefore, I feel it's best to let them make their calls and read their messages, and be either in or out of the room, rather than trying to do both at the same time.

Here's what I say. "I know that you are all busy and that you have many demands on your time. I also know that you are here right now because at this moment, this is the most important place for you to be. When we take a break I will tell you the time that I will restart. If you're not back at that time I will presume that you have something more important that you need to do. I'm happy with that, because I want to make sure that when you're out of the room it's because you have to do something that is more important for you, which is fine by me, and when you're in the room you can be 100% focussed on what we're working on here. I will restart at the time I say, whether you're here or not.

By lunchtime on the first day of my most recent Master Practitioner training, the entire group were back on time from breaks, and one of the students commented later in the week that he had never seen such a well behaved training group!

Of course, for this to work, you have to be disciplined. You have to be back on time and set the right example. The simplest way to do this, which might sound a bit antisocial, is to avoid your students at break times! They will often want to engage you in deep and meaningful conversations, and it's easy to lose track of time. Also, remember that break times and lunch time are your breaks as well as theirs. Take time to gather your thoughts and plan your next session, and always be in the room waiting for them to return.

At the time you've said you'll start, start. Some of the group might still be settling down and finishing conversations. It's a question of priorities, and at the beginning I have said that "when you're in the room you can be 100% focussed", so if you're in the room, pay attention, and if you aren't ready to do that then be outside of the room.

The choice is always with my students, because I can't control what they are doing and what other distractions are going on in their lives. I can only deliver the best training that I can, on time, to whoever chooses to be in the room.

It can't be that simple, can it? Well, taking a clear line on timekeeping and engagement will prevent the majority of problems from occurring, because your students will quickly learn that you mean what you say. What you then may need to do, in extreme cases, is correct any behaviours which you feel are disruptive to your group.

Here's my suggestion for how you might do that.

Don't wait for the right moment to talk to someone, because someone who is being deliberately disruptive will never allow themselves to be on their own where you might corner them, so they will always be in the middle of really important conversations. If you don't assert your leadership, you might as well pack up and go home, because the disruptive student is now leading the group.

As soon as you observe something that you want to put right, directly ask the student to join your for a private conversation. I find, "Have you got a minute?" is sufficient, and on rare occasions, "Let's have a quick chat. Yes, now." Then, once you have them alone, tell them clearly, concisely and directly:

1. This is how you are behaving

2. This is how that is unacceptable

3. If you continue, this is what will happen

You're not inviting a conversation, you're not asking their permission. It's your course, your group, your rules.

Therefore, you must not conclude with a submissive statement such as, "Is that OK?" because it's not up to them, it's up to you.

Most importantly, if they do continue, and some people will definitely push their luck if they see you being soft on other points such as timekeeping, you need to actually do the thing that you said you would do. Therefore, be extremely cautious about making threats which you will not follow through. If you threaten to remove them from the course then you fail to do that, they have won and you might as well pack up and go home. If this sounds like a power struggle then that's exactly what it is, driven by the power of their fears and insecurities. What they want is security and safety, and the way that they will get that is by respecting your authority. For them to win control of the group is a poor second for them, because they won't know what to do with it once they have it. They would much rather you be in charge.

There's one final thing that I tell the whole group to create a foundation for dealing with such issues.

"Some of you are going to have odd reactions to the techniques we're working on because your old fears will surface and you'll behave in ways that you didn't expect. You have to remember, that's not you, that's your fear and insecurity. We all have them, and the only thing that I can promise you is that you will never have a better opportunity than this week to address those issues. You will never be surrounded by such a highly skilled group of people who care about you, who are here to help and support you, in this environment where we have all the time we need for you to get all the things that are most important to you in your life. Remember, you will never have a better opportunity than you have this week to achieve that."

You will absolutely need to be clear with any disruptive students that their behaviour is not acceptable, and you can then end the conversation with an insight into why they are behaving in that way, and an offer of help. My experience is that no-one is just disruptive for the sake of it, they are trying to achieve something for themselves which they don't know how to achieve in any other way, and they often feel backed into a corner, so they act from fear rather than rational thought.

Hang on, did I just say that they want to achieve something for themselves? Well of course! There is a positive intention motivating every behaviour... and a context in which every behaviour has value.

As I often say to corporate managers – their employees can turn up late for work, they can spend all day on Facebook, they can go home early. That's their choice and it's absolutely fine. They just need to do that somewhere else.

14 Society of NLP Certification Criteria

14.1   Society of NLP

The following criteria for NLP
Practitioner and NLP Master
Practitioner certification are
determined by the Society of
NLP, the original NLP licensing
body which was first formed in
1979, the year in which
Bandler and Grinder's first NLP
book, "Frogs into Princes" was
published.

When you attend a certified training program, you will need
to sign a license agreement which ensures that you
understand the rights and obligations of certification. You
can request a copy of the agreement by emailing me at
learn@nenlp.com.

14.2   NLP Practitioner

14.2.1   Representational Systems

Detect signs and sequences of representational systems

Detect submodalities in all representational systems

Change sequences of representational systems

Access information in all representational systems

Communicate in all representational systems

Translate between representational systems

Detect simultaneous and sequential incongruities

14.2.2   Rapport Building

Establish rapport in all representational systems

14.2.3   Pace and Lead

Pace and lead non-verbally and verbally

Pace and lead through mirroring, direct matching and indirect matching in all representational systems

14.2.4   Anchoring

Elicit and install anchors in all representational systems

Stacking, amplify, collapse and chain anchors

Disassociation techniques including the Phobia Cure and future-pacing

14.2.5   Language Patterns

Detect and use the patterns of the Meta Model and Milton Model as information-gathering and information-organizing tools.

14.2.6   Outcome Orientation

Set well-formed outcomes

14.2.7   Reframing

Use basic reframing techniques

Six Step Reframing

14.2.8   Sub-Modalities

Swish

Timeline

14.2.9   Strategies

Basic strategy elicitation skills

14.2.10   Trance

Basic trance induction and utilisation procedures

Trance induction using the Meta Model and Milton Model language patterns

14.3   NLP Master Practitioner

Multi-level tasking and purposeful multi-level communication, including:

Detect conscious and unconscious communication.

Distinguish between content and structure.

Understand and integrate the presuppositions of NLP.

Understand remedial and generative change.

Customising NLP Practitioner techniques to meet the needs of a client.

Creating states of consciousness and physiology that lead to flexibility and creativity in thinking and action.

Making conscious shifts in perspective, state and behaviour to maintain overall control of the coaching process.

14.3.1　Meta Programs

Elicit Meta Programs and build them into your coaching approach.

14.3.2　Framing outcomes

Understand the difference between an outcome and a direction.

Have a systemic approach to predicting the implications of change over time.

Generalise change through time.

14.3.3　Advanced Language Skills

Detect Sleight of Mouth Patterns.

Reframing at different logical levels using the various Sleight of Mouth Patterns.

Sort incongruities and integrate them conversationally.

Implement the patterns of NLP techniques conversationally, e.g. through presuppositions in questions.

14.3.4　Values and Criteria

Elicit values for the purpose of motivation, setting outcomes, negotiation procedures, conflict resolution, etc.

14.3.5　Advanced Strategies Skills

Elicit, design, modify and install strategies.

Use motivation, convincer, decision, and follow through strategies inside other techniques.

14.3.6 Trance

Recognise, induce, and utilise naturally occurring trance phenomena, also known as conversational hypnosis.

Developing a greater awareness and utilisation of a systemic approach.

14.4 NLP Trainer

14.4.1 Certification Requirements

Certification as a NLP Practitioner.

Certification as a NLP Master Practitioner.

Certification as a NLP Trainer Associate.

Hypnosis Training, emphasizing Ericksonian Hypnosis.

Assistant on a complete NLP Practitioner Program and a complete Master Practitioner Program.

A minimum of 100 hours of teaching/training experience, which must include teaching NLP.

A solid understanding of NLP Operational Presuppositions, Representational Systems, Rapport, Anchoring, basic Milton Model Patterns and fundamental induction and utilization processes, Meta Model Patterns, Outcome Frame and Well-formedness Conditions, basic Strategy modeling processes, Reframing (Content, Context and 6-Step Reframing, Sub-Modalities (including the Visual Squash and the Swish Pattern), as well as other basic NLP Techniques (including Changing Past Personal History, Phobia Cure).

Written Test.

DVD of the first hour of a presentation or training with a new group, accompanied by a written planning outline of the presentation, including a written description of the first two exercises, including any handouts.

Certification fee of U.S. $300, upon the completion of all NLP Trainer requirements. (In 2016)

14.4.2   Competencies

Engage in multi-level tasking, e.g., purposeful multi-level communication.

Detect the differences between conscious and unconscious mind communication.

Make the distinction between content and the form of the content.

Integrate the NLP operational presuppositions into their thinking (attitude) and behavior.

Know the difference between remedial and generative change.

Combine the various elements of the techniques to design customized interventions.

Build and utilize states of consciousness and physiology leading to greater flexibility, variability, creativity and mobility in thinking and in action.

Make conscious shifts in perspective, state and behavior (e.g., re-sequence habitual representational system sequences to interrupt states perceived as "unresourceful") to keep open opportunities for discovery, creativity and learning for yourself and others.

Utilize linguistic skills defined by purpose, e.g., use of language in ways that demonstrate "conversational interventions."

Develop a greater awareness and application of a systemic approach.

INPUT ACUITY SKILLS consist of the ability to detect, that is, to use senses with agility and flexibility, increasing the range of what you are able to perceive in all sensory systems. The verb "to detect" is operationally defined as the ability to identify and make sensory-based discriminations.

Detect representational systems and sequences of representational systems through the set of physiological phenomena collectively referred to as "representational system accessing cues."

Make discriminations in all major input channels: Visual, Auditory tonal and digital, Kinesthetic and their sub-modality distinctions.

Detect and make the distinction between simultaneous and sequential incongruities; make the distinction between unfamiliarity and discomfort, agreement and understanding.

Detect the differences in the form of conscious and unconscious mind communication.

Language Patterns: Detect the linguistic distinctions known collectively as the Meta Model, Milton Model, which includes presuppositions, ambiguities and temporal distinctions; the ability to detect the linguistic markers that presuppose Meta Program reference structures; the ability to detect the class of language known as Sleight of Mouth Patterns.

INTERNAL REPRESENTATION SKILLS consist of the ability to use your internal processes with agility

and flexibility. Internal requisite variety is operationally defined as the ability to do the following:

Represent information in all sensory systems.

Access information from and in each representational system.

Store information in all systems.

Overlap with facility and ease from each representational system into another.

Make sub-modality distinctions in all primary representational systems and re-sequence characteristic representational system sequences to build a solid foundation of resource and choice.

Access states and physiology that promote flexibility and variability in thinking and behavior which are independent of the three obstacles to learning and teaching, according to NLP Co-Developer, John Grinder: (1) internal dialogue at too high a volume; (2) tunnel vision (i.e., only seeing what is in the center of your visual field and failing to notice and recognize the relational aspects in the environment; (3) unnecessary tension in the body.

The over-all purpose of developing, expanding and enhancing these abilities is to create greater flexibility, creativity and mobility in thinking; the ability to make conscious shifts in perspective, internal state and behavior that open up new channels of discovery, learning and change for yourself and your participants.

OUTPUT SKILLS: Utilization Skills include modeling skills, rapport-building skills, anchoring skills,

language skills and multi-level communication, design and presentation skills that utilize conscious and unconscious mind learning strategies, meta-linguistic awareness (the ability to think about language and comment on language).

Output flexibility is operationally defined as the ability to do the following:

Vary behavior in all output communication channels.

Establish rapport at both conscious and unconscious levels, demonstrating the ability to use mirroring, direct matching and indirect matching (i.e., cross-over mirroring).; pace and lead in each and all representational systems, verbally and non-verbally, including: whole and part body postures, breathing patterns, intonation patterns, sensory-system predicate usage sequences of eye accessing cues, and sub-modality accessing cues and gestures

Utilize the patterns of the Meta Model, Well-Formed Outcome Frame, Milton Model and "Sleight of Mouth" patterns (Patterns of Reformulation) to gather and organize information in ways that expand the range of possibility and choice in thinking and in action.

Adjust one's language and behavior to pace the structure of another person's experience in relation of Meta Programs; also appropriately adjust (i.e., balance) the configuration of Meta Programs.

Sort incongruities, polarities and "double-bind," either-or thinking patterns and reintegrate them in ways that expand the range of what's possible.

Elicit and anchor states (resources) in each and all representational systems, i.e., kinesthetically,

auditorily and visually; directionalize and contextualize states using the basic anchoring formats: setting and utilizing spatial anchors, stacking anchors, amplifying anchors, collapsing or synchronizing anchors, and chaining (or sequencing) responses

Demonstrate strategy elicitation, design and installation, including criteria; the ability to detect and utilize the following key strategies: internal performance strategies, motivational strategies, decision strategies, and learning strategies.

Structure and implement "testing" procedures in consideration of ecological implications of change through time to "preserve" the integrity of the system as a whole.

Identify the structure and function of each technique; appropriate contextualization and generalization of change techniques; re-anchoring formats, reframing techniques and basic negotiation models, sub-modality technology, threshold patterns, Swish Patterns; and Future-Pacing techniques.

14.5   Trainer Competencies Explained

The list of required competencies for certification as a NLP Trainer is quite detailed, so I'll revisit the list and give you some further suggestions for how you can develop the required skills.

You'll notice that many of these competencies are duplicated from the Practitioner and Master Practitioner certification requirements, and I've pointed out where this is the case. If you are already a competent Master Practitioner, you really don't have much to worry about.

Engage in multi-level tasking, e.g., purposeful multi-level communication.

This is a Master Practitioner competency. Talk to the client at the same time as figuring out where to go next.

Detect the differences between conscious and unconscious mind communication.

This is a Master Practitioner competency. Typically, verbal versus non-verbal communication.

Make the distinction between content and the form of the content.

This is a Master Practitioner competency. Content is what happened, structure or form is how it happened.

Integrate the NLP operational presuppositions into their thinking (attitude) and behavior.

This is a Practitioner competency. Read the presuppositions and make sure you form your own understanding of them.

Know the difference between remedial and generative change.

Another Practitioner competency. Creating choices rather than fixing problems.

Combine the various elements of the techniques to design customized interventions.

This is a Practitioner competency and you should have moved beyond this already at Master Practitioner level. By the time you're training as a NLP Trainer, you should be way past techniques.

Build and utilize states of consciousness and physiology leading to greater flexibility ...

This is a Master Practitioner competency. Get your client to think and do things which get them to move.

Make conscious shifts in perspective, state and behavior ... to keep open opportunities for discovery, creativity and learning ...

Out-think your clients to get around the obstacles that they create.

Utilize linguistic skills defined by purpose ...

Use NLP techniques conversationally, a Master Practitioner competency.

Develop a greater awareness and application of a systemic approach.

A systemic approach takes into account the system or environment that your client is operating within.

INPUT ACUITY SKILLS ...

Pay attention to your clients. Personally, I don't advocate developing your 'sensory acuity' to notice every twitch of an eyebrow, it's a waste of your time and resources. Instead, you need to be ahead of your clients, not trying to keep up with them.

Detect representational systems and sequences ...

This is another Practitioner level competency – tracking a client's strategies from their language and behaviour.

Make discriminations in all major input channels: Visual, Auditory tonal and digital, Kinesthetic and their sub-modality distinctions.

Submodalities – another Practitioner competency.

Detect and make the distinction between simultaneous and sequential incongruities ...

Another Practitioner competency, with a focus on mind reading the student's learning state.

Detect the differences in the form of conscious and unconscious mind communication.

This is an interesting competency, because many experts argue that there is no such distinction, that there is no conscious or unconscious mind, only a mind and a focus of awareness within that. How we can therefore tell the difference between conscious and unconscious communication could perhaps be defined as being able to tell the difference between what they client says and what they mean, or what they communicate without knowing. In any case, this is a Master Practitioner competency.

Language Patterns ... Meta Model, Milton Model ... Meta Program ... Sleight of Mouth Patterns.

A set of Master Practitioner competencies, and Sleight of Mouth which I have discussed with the owner of the SNLP as being irrelevant because it is a super-set of Meta Model, and she agreed with me. Therefore, if you have a Practitioner level understanding of Meta and Milton Models then that's good enough.

INTERNAL REPRESENTATION SKILLS ...

These are all Practitioner competencies.

Represent information in all sensory systems.

Pay attention to not just what you see and hear.

Access information from and in each representational system.

Pay attention to not just what you see and hear.

Store information in all systems.

Pay attention to not just what you see and hear.

Overlap with facility and ease from each representational system into another.

Overlapping is when you use metaphors from a different representational system, for example if the client says "bright", you would use "loud" as an auditory metaphor so that you could avoid directly referring to the visual elements.

Make sub-modality distinctions ...

Use strategies to support the learning process.

Access states and physiology that promote flexibility and variability in thinking and behavior which are independent of the three obstacles to learning and teaching, according to NLP Co-Developer, John Grinder ...

Be flexible to get round three barriers to learning: the student's own self-talk, the student's focus being to narrow and the student being tense. Of course, there may be many more barriers to learning.

The over-all purpose ... is to create greater flexibility, creativity and mobility in thinking ...

Keep one step ahead of your students.

OUTPUT SKILLS ...

Behave in a way that makes use of all of the skills you've developed through learning NLP. You're not only a Trainer, you're also still a Master Practitioner and a Practitioner. The skill sets are each different and complementary.

Output flexibility is operationally defined as the ability to do the following:

Vary behavior in all output communication channels.

Be flexible in both your words and actions. If you're one step ahead of your students, you actually don't need to be flexible anyway!

Establish rapport at both conscious and unconscious levels ...

This is a Practitioner level competency. Actually, a whole bunch of competencies based on paying attention to your client and utilising what they give you.

Utilize the patterns of the Meta Model, Well-Formed Outcome Frame, Milton Model and "Sleight of Mouth" patterns ...

Use your Master Practitioner skills to negotiate around any learning barriers.

Adjust one's language and behavior to pace the structure of another person's experience in relation of Meta Programs ...

Use your Master Practitioner skills to negotiate around any learning barriers.

Sort incongruities, polarities and "double-bind," either-or thinking patterns and reintegrate them in ways that expand the range of what's possible.

Use your Master Practitioner skills to negotiate around any learning barriers.

Elicit and anchor states (resources) in each and all representational systems ...

Anchoring is fundamentally a learning technique, so if you know how to anchor reliably, you'll be able to use anchors to support the learning process.

Demonstrate strategy elicitation, design and installation ...

If you know what makes your students 'tick', you can be more effective in supporting their learning. This is a Master Practitioner competency.

Structure and implement "testing" procedures ...

This is essentially the Master Practitioner criteria of "Have a systemic approach to predicting the implications of change over time."

Identify the structure and function of each technique ...

Know your Practitioner and Master Practitioner techniques inside-out. If you don't, how can you teach them?

14.6 Simplified Trainer Competencies

If we remove the competencies which you have already demonstrated in order to achieve your Practitioner and Master Practitioner certification (assuming that your trainer was competent!) then we have the following new criteria for Trainer certification.

Make conscious shifts in perspective, state and behavior ...

Out-think your students to get around their obstacles.

Overlap with facility and ease from each representational system

Use metaphors from different representational systems

Make sub-modality distinctions ... re-sequence ...

Use strategies to support the learning process.

Access states and physiology that promote flexibility and variability in thinking and behavior ...

Be flexible to get round three barriers to learning.

Vary behavior in all output communication channels.

Be flexible in both your words and actions.

Elicit and anchor states ...

Anchoring is a Practitioner competency, however there's a bit more to it at Trainer level.

Identify the structure and function of each technique ...

Know your Practitioner and Master Practitioner techniques inside-out. If you don't, how can you teach them?

---

15 Assessment

As a NLP Trainer, you have a duty to uphold the certification criteria and standards of the Society of NLP, or whatever your chosen licensing organisation is.

Even if you're not certifying your students, you still have a duty to give them what they paid for, and to ensure that, you must have some form of assessment.

Perhaps over 90% of the NLP trainers I've ever seen have conducted no form of assessment at all, so the certificate cannot be a certificate of achievement, it can only be a certificate of attendance. If you've paid a lot of money to train in something like NLP, don't you want to be recognised for more than just being in the room?

I've asked other trainers about this over the years, and they tell me that they are observing and evaluating their students on an ongoing basis. No they're not. Ask them how many students have ever not received a certificate. Failing students can be uncomfortable, but if you don't apply your success criteria consistently, then your certification and your training mean nothing. You might as well just sell certificates.

I attended a NLP Business Practitioner course back in 2002, run by an extremely well known trainer. At the end of the course, our certificates were given out and the trainer had the whole group of 200 people place the certificates on their heads and repeat a frankly demeaning and insulting statement about promising to use our NLP skills wisely. That one act negated the entire certification process.

In this chapter I will therefore explain a bit about assessment and also share with you how I assess students on NLP Practitioner and Master Practitioner courses.

15.1   Practitioner Assessment

Here's how I introduce the Practitioner assessment day.

For each session you'll be told who you are working with and the pairs are drawn up on a random rotation so that everyone has an equal share of being practitioner and client, and everyone works with someone different each time.

In order to give you as much practice time as possible, the timing of this last day is very important. The session start times will be displayed in the room and at the start of each session you'll be told when to be back in the room.

It's easy to get wrapped up in these sessions and want to carry on all day with one person. If you don't stick to the times given, you are denying yourself the quality practice that you need in order to fully integrate the skills you've learned throughout the course, and of course you are also missing out on the opportunity to receive feedback that may be vital in achieving Practitioner certification.

It's very common that at the start of the day, delegates have an armful of tools and techniques that they know how to use, but they don't know how to choose. This is one of the key outcomes of the day. As you work through the sessions, you will probably find yourself talking much less and listening much more.

Remembering that the client will tell you everything you need to know in the first few sentences, you'll soon find that listening to the client and getting a sense of the structure of the problem or situation will give you all the information you need to choose your approach.

15.1.1 Client

As a client, you have the opportunity to work on some issues that are really important to you. You may have a fear that you want to tackle or a problem to solve. Many people who come to the Practitioner course are running their own businesses - or thinking about it - and this is an ideal opportunity to do some serious planning with the help of a talented group of coaches.

You can spend some time planning the issues or opportunities you are going to explore during the sessions so that you can get the most value from the time. You will learn as much about the process as the client as you will as the Practitioner, so both roles are equally important.

15.1.2 Practitioner

At first, many people find they are so busy thinking about which technique to use that they miss what the client tells them. After a while, they find that spending at least half the time just listening and exploring the issue is time well spent.

As a Practitioner, perhaps your most important job is to maintain an outcome oriented state. You can use all of your rapport skills to lead your client and in many cases, all the Practitioner has to do is sit there and look confident while the client finds their own solution!

NLP's techniques are each built around a particular structure, so by exploring the structure of the problem, you'll be able to choose the most appropriate technique.

Here are a few examples techniques that you can use and situations where they might be relevant.

Anchoring	To capture useful states or integrate states, and to control and test responses
Fast phobia cure	For a situation where the client's undesired response is too strong for them
Future pace	Creating the possibility for change
Meta model	Always vital when exploring and mapping out the issue being presented
Milton model	To gently guide the client towards their desired outcome
Modelling	Model the problem and elicit its strategy
Outcomes	To find out what the client wants!
Pattern interrupt	To interrupt an undesirable state
Rapport	To non-verbally guide the client towards the desired outcome
Rapport	To guide the communication process
Six step reframe	For repetitive patterns of behaviour
Storytelling	To change state or shape an outcome
Submodalities	Exploring perceptual distortions
Swish	For habitual behaviours and reactions
Timeline	To explore a future decision or set goals
Trance	To help the client explore in a relaxed way, free from distractions

It's worth remembering that the technique will be less effective if you concentrate only on the technique. It's best to think about how you'll use the whole time to deliver the technique more elegantly. Here's a simple process you can use if you need to:

State Choose a resourceful state Outcomes Set a direction Rapport Get into rapport Questions Learn about the problem Intervention The technique! Future pace Create a future where the problem is solved Test Check to make sure the intervention worked

There may be times when you get stuck and don't know where to go next - that's fine. It often happens as a result of the Practitioner thinking too much about the technique. Here are some ideas for what you can say or ask when you get stuck.

- That's right

- What would be a good outcome for you in this?

- Where do you believe you are right now on this?

- What would you like to do next?

Finally, and perhaps most importantly, the practice sessions are not a test. There is no right or wrong course of action and what I am looking for is that you are able to help the client move in the general direction they want to go. I don't really care if a technique appears to work or not - they don't always work for me! What I'm most interested in seeing is you acting in the interests of your client, maintaining your state and making the most of the opportunity to develop your skills.

15.2   Master Practitioner Assessment

For Master Practitioner, what I want to assess is the students' ability to model a talent. I want to see that they can identify the behaviour of a talent, Meta Model the structure of that behaviour, abstract that structure into a model and then install that model by teaching it to other students. Finally, I want to see them test the model by getting their installation subjects to replicate the behaviour. All of that takes place in half a day.

Other trainers send students away to conduct a modelling project, and here's the problem with that – the students will preselect people who they think have the talent they're looking for. This contradicts one of the presuppositions of NLP, that the client has all the resources they need to effect a change. Whatever talent you're interested in, everyone has it.

Not everyone can play a musical instrument, but that's not a talent, that's a learned behaviour. Being presented with three modelling subjects who you have not selected yourself forces students to look for that talent within that person, and encourages them to choose talents which are definable behaviours.

The rota works in the same way as for Practitioner, so each student will model three subjects and then have time to create their model and their installation. When their design time is up, the students take it in turns to demonstrate their installation and answer questions about their overall approach and findings.

You will need to make sure that your students are choosing realistic behaviours to model, so ask them to think of a modelling topic a day or two before the assessment and make time to review their choices. If they choose something like 'leadership' or 'influence' then simply ask, "Is that a behaviour?"

If the topic is too broad, there will be too many behavioural steps, too many variables and they will not create a meaningful model in the time available. The more specific they are, the more value they will get from the exercise.

Students on my most recent Master Practitioner program chose subjects such as, "How to like a food that you don't currently like", "How to start haggling to get a better price" and "How to choose ingredients for a meal from what is already in the kitchen". Interesting, eh?

At the time that they choose the behaviour they want to model, they will not know who they will be working with, because you will not have shared the rota at that point. Therefore, their choice must be based on something that they are interested in, rather that something that they think that someone is good at. When we're modelling, we don't know what we're looking for at first and we have to figure that out through careful cross-referencing.

When I model high performers in business, I ask for three high performers and three average so that I can cross-reference and discard the aspects of the model which are not relevant to high performance. With three random subjects, your students are very likely to find a range of abilities with which to cross-reference.

15.3   Rota

I highly recommend that you do not allow your students to choose their own partners for the assessment sessions, because they will choose the people they want to work with, which doesn't reflect 'real life', and they will end up not having a fair balance of sessions as Practitioner and Client.

Here's the rota which I use. While this will cater for up to 8 students, you can split a larger group and use the same rota for each sub-group. You would need either 4 or 8 sessions to fully rotate the groups, so I have found over the years that this format is the most practical, because in reality I don't think you need more than 6 sessions. This also neatly fits into a morning, including a briefing and a good break, and everyone can breathe a sigh of relief and enjoy their lunch.

This works for both Practitioner and Master Practitioner.

Session	1	2	3	Break	4	5	6
Time	09:30	10:00	10:30	11:00	11:30	12:00	12:30
Coach	A	B	A		B	A	B
Client	B	E	D		G	F	C
Coach	C	D	C		D	C	D
Client	D	G	F		A	H	E
Coach	E	F	E		F	E	F
Client	F	A	H		C	B	G
Coach	G	H	G		H	G	H
Client	H	C	B		E	D	A

15.4   Trainer Assessment

The most obvious activity for a NLP Trainer assessment is to run a training session, however this raises some problems, the most obvious of which is the duration. Getting a student to deliver a 20 minute demo session is not the same as delivering even a half day of training. Staying on time, managing students, delivering demonstrations, managing practice sessions, none of this is a problem for a 20 minute session.

The job of a trainer is not to stand at the front of the room and talk. It is to manage a complete and well-structured learning experience, and you're unlikely to see evidence of that in a 20 minute demo.

Your SNLP Trainer Training certification requires you to send in a video of the first hour of your Practitioner training, along with a description of your course design. That gives me a sense of the way you've approached the design process and allows me to see how your exercises connect together within a larger structure. Of course, it also allows me to see that you're actually covering the required certification criteria for your Practitioner and Master Practitioner training.

15.5   Assessment Criteria

The most obvious thing that I can tell you about assessment is that you have to actually be observing your students in order to know if they have met your criteria or not. If you were paying a lot of money to attend a training course like this, wouldn't you want to know that, a) you had earned the certificate and, b) the assessment actually meant something because you could give specific feedback on their performance?

If you have multiple pairs of students conducting their assessment sessions at the same time, you obviously can't observe them all together. Therefore, you also need to plan your own time so that you see everyone at least open and close a session.

In addition to the SNLP criteria, you will also need to decide what your own additional criteria are. For example, do you want to see evidence of the session having a clearly defined start and end? If you're giving a 'five minute warning' then your students have no excuse not to wrap their sessions up neatly, even if they haven't finished a technique as they intended.

What will be more important to you, performing a technique 'by the book' or maintaining a productive relationship with the client?

The SNLP criteria are the minimum baseline for assessment, so you need to share these with your students prior to the start of the course, so that they know what to focus on. Above that, your own additional criteria define the experience you want to create in your training.

15.6   Pass or Fail?

Once you have worked out your standards for assessment, you then have to face the issue of what to do when a student does not meet your criteria.

Let's be straight, I have never met another NLP Trainer who fails students. In my view, this devalues the certification, because all that a student has to do to pass is turn up to the training. 15 years ago, I attended a Business Practitioner run by someone who used to co-train with Bandler. After the afternoon tea break on the final day, all 200 students went back into the training room to find our certificates waiting for us. The trainer had us put them on our heads and recite something about promising not to be 'assholes' (he was American). It was a farce, a ludicrous insult to the value of the certificate. If you don't have to earn something, if there is no standard for pass or fail, how can you feel proud of what you've achieved? Do you feel proud for tuning up and sitting in a chair for 8 days?

This is why it's so important for you to set your standards, right now. When you're looking into the doleful eyes of a student who expects to hear good news, it's too late to figure out what your standards are. If you know now, you can offer meaningful feedback throughout the training process.

Trainers who don't fail students tell me that they continuously monitor their students' progress and give developmental feedback. I've seen a few trainers in action, and I've seen no evidence of this.

Development feedback is critical, specific and negative. A lot of trainers don't like to be critical, specific or negative, so they like to give positive feedback about what their students are doing well. That's nice, but it doesn't help anyone to improve. Knowing what I did right is only half the story. I must also know what I did wrong. Only when I have both sets of information can I self correct.

15.6.1   HELPful Feedback

To make life easier for you when giving feedback, I've devised a little framework and mnemonic to HELP you.

We all present an image to the world, an image of perfection, of how we want to be seen and judged by others. Even someone who says, "I don't care what other people think of me" is presenting an image.

We believe that the image that we present is all that people see, our 'light' side, and that we are very good at hiding our faults, mistakes, bad habits and evil thoughts from others, our 'dark' side.

In our dark side, we hide our fears and insecurities. We hide the mistakes we make and the aspects of ourselves that we think of as bad or negative, but we only judge ourselves this way because we have learned to. In reality, behaviour is neither good nor bad, it is only effective at getting the result, or not.

Without mistakes and failures, we have no source of feedback to correct ourselves. If you're trying to navigate in the car, what happens when you take a wrong turn? Do you stop immediately and refuse to drive any further? Do you blame someone else for giving you the wrong directions? Do you blame the road signs? Or do you simply turn around and correct your mistake?

Feedback is neutral, it's just information. We attach judgement and meaning to the feedback, so we learn to seek out 'good' feedback and avoid 'bad' feedback. We learn that feedback is a judgement on our value as a person.

Of course, this is ridiculous. When you were a child, you didn't know any better, but you're not a child any more. Whether you see feedback as a criticism, or praise, or a weakness, or a strength, what you are actually doing is distorting the feedback. You are changing the feedback so that it confirms what you already know. If you believe that you are weak, you will hear feedback as a weakness. If you believe that you are strong, you will hear feedback as a strength. It is neither, and the only danger is in the judgement, the distortion.

Our brains, like many of the automated systems that you rely on every day, are 'servo systems', they direct behaviour towards a goal. Imagine a toy car which has a very simply arrangement of a motor, wheels and some kind of sensor to direct it towards a target. The car's guidance system doesn't need to be accurate, it only needs to keep focus on the target. The car's path will look something like this:

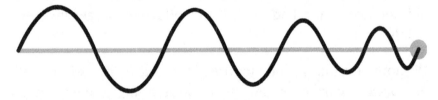

The car is 'off course' for most of its journey, yet it still gets there. That's what your behaviour is like as you direct yourself towards your goals. Sometimes, it will feel like you're moving backwards, but that doesn't matter. What matters is that you are moving.

Of course, we don't simply head towards our goals, because we have other forces that act upon us. Most of us can't head off to a tropical island whenever we want, we have jobs to do and bills to pay, so we find a way to balance our lives. If we don't weigh up the different aspects of every goal, we ignore some of the factors that could lead to failure, with the result that we don't end up where we wanted to be.

The past and the future are illusions, tricks that we play on ourselves to explain where we are right now and to give us a sense of control over our lives. The past and future are lies. We change the past to suit ourselves, and we pretend that the future will definitely happen, just because we think it will. The only truth is in the present moment, and what you can do right now.

Feedback is part of any servo system, a system that self corrects to achieve a specific goal. Here's a simple method to help you avoid the judgement that leads to the emotional resistance that will prevent you from giving the best chance for your students to succeed.

H	What **Happened**	Say or show what happened without judging it as good or bad
E	What you **Expected**	State or show the point of reference, the intended result
L	Don't **Leave** it	Give the feedback as quickly as you can
P	Make it **Personal**	Only what you saw, heard or felt. Second hand feedback is subjective

For example, "I saw that you started your swish with the desired outcome and replaced it with the 'problem', the swish works by pacing the 'problem' and leading into the new outcome."

Give feedback on what you observe directly, not what you hear second hand, not what you 'feel', not what 'seems to you'. By presenting hard evidence, you allow your student to self-correct.

It's also important to give feedback as soon as you observe the behaviour that you want to influence.

The most important point about this method is that you aren't telling the student what to do – you're merely pointing out the difference between what they did and what you expected them to do.

Note that you can equally use the exact same framework for giving positive feedback. "I saw that you spent most of your time locating the trigger for the response, that's exactly right, and it will make the swish much more effective."

Remember that whatever your students do is neither good nor bad, it simply gets them closer to your outcome or not. They can do the swish any way they like, but the more they deviate from what you've demonstrated, the less likely they are to achieve a 'result'. You can encourage them to test and experiment – that's a great source of feedback too.

15.6.1.1   HELP!

Give your 'students' an exercise to practice and give them feedback using the HELP formula.

¹⁶ The End

How are you going to conclude your training?

We talked about how you open your training, and how this creates your learners' expectations and their frame of reference for what comes next. Should the end of your training be any different? After all, the end of one chapter is merely the beginning of the next.

You could close with some kind of ceremony, such as handing out certificates, but this is divisive if not all of your learners have met the certification criteria. Therefore, until you have assessed them, you might want to give yourself the option of either having a certification ceremony or not. They won't know what you had planned anyway!

Certainly you'll want to close any open loops and get your learners to step back and reflect on the whole experience. Metaphorical activities work well for this, such as shared creative exercises where the learners collaborate to produce a visual metaphor for their journey.

It's a very easy way to close off the course, it's relaxing, fun, engaging and everyone gets to showcase their own personal experience and creativity.

You could use one big piece of paper which everyone contributes to, or you could start with individual pieces which they each draw and write on, and then have to fit them all together into a giant puzzle before finally commenting as a group on the patterns and the connections that they can see.

Make sure that you allow plenty of time for drawing, and also for each individual to share their thoughts on their metaphor and their experiences with the group.

Here's an example of some individual small pieces of paper arranged on the floor of a training room. You can see a pile of coloured pens in the middle of the circle, so that the learners are forced to stay together and share the pens, even though they are working on individual metaphors.

And here's an example of an individual metaphor on a piece of large paper.

Finally, here's an example of what a group contribution might look like.

If you just ask your learners to talk about what they have learned, you risk getting only shallow reflections along the lines of "I learned how to put on a play". What you really need is for your learners to step back and reflect on their learning from a higher, more abstract level.

One way to do this is to explicitly ask them to do it!

For example, think of something that you remember from your training, then think about what that means to you, then think about what that does for you, and so on.

Each question builds on the one before and the sequence leads your learners to shift their awareness and bring in more aspects of their experience in order to formulate an answer.

Let's try an example.

16.1.1.1 Abstracting Learning

Think of something that you remember from this book, or from your NLP Trainer Training experience.

Take a minute or two to carefully consider each question.

When you recall that, what do you notice about it?

And as you notice what you recall, what does that mean to you?

And as you consider what that means to you, how is that important for you?

And as you discover how that is important for you, how is that valuable for you?

And as you realise how that is valuable for you, what does all of this mean that you have truly learned?

And as you find what you have truly learned, what can this mean for you in the future, moving forwards?

And as you can see what this means for you in the future, moving forwards, where does this new learning lead you?

And as you explore where this new learning leads you, what does all of this do for you, and for the work that you do?

And finally, thinking carefully about all of this, where are you now in your learning journey, as you realise these new abilities that you can enjoy?

Let's think back to what we have learned about learning. Firstly, the learning cycle. To ensure the efficient integration of new knowledge and behaviours, we must follow a sequence of Concrete Experience, Reflective Observation, Abstract Concept and Active Experimentation. How can you build this into your closing activities to support the learning process?

Secondly, consider the different types of learning theories that we explored:

- Behavioural

- Cognitive

- Constructivist

- Social

We must ensure that our closing activities, and the integration of the learning process, gives our learners something to do, some knowledge to acquire, something to create and has an element of group interaction.

What would happen if we simply gave our learners these ingredients and asked them to design their own closing activity? Would knowledge of the design process change the result?

16.1.1.2   Design Your Final Scene

Create your own closing activity.

Incorporate at least one cycle of: Concrete Experience, Reflective Observation, Abstract Concept and Active Experimentation.

Incorporate the following learning models: Behavioural (Do something without understanding why), Cognitive (Understand why), Constructivist (Create something) and Social (Interact within a group).

Once you've designed your activity, test it with a group.

Finally, consider what you want to say to your learners as they head home.

- Thank you

- You've been a wonderful audience

- Come again

- Remember to exit through the gift shop

16.1.1.3   Closing Words

What are the closing words that you want to share with your learners?

An inspiring quote or story? Perhaps some instructions?

Note some ideas here.

The NLP Trainer Training Manual

17 The Beginning

During your journey through NLP training, what have you discovered about NLP, and in that exploration, discovered about yourself?

You may remember the words of one of NLP's co-creators, Richard Bandler: "NLP is an attitude and a methodology which leaves behind a trail of techniques".

You have now spent some time exploring those techniques, and at this point, some of them may seem unimpressive, others miraculous, and this is an insight into the subjective nature of ourselves. If we could guarantee that a particular technique would work before you had even met the person you're working with, life would be without its rich diversity and exciting challenges. All of the footprints would look the same, and would all lead to the same place.

As you have explored NLP, you have added your own footprints to this journey that we share.

As you develop your ideas and integrate the principles of NLP with the skills and experience that you already have even further, you will serve as a guide to others hoping to make that journey that is our birthright; the journey of self discovery, insight and knowledge.

Some people find NLP through a desire to help others, and some people have something that they want for themselves. Whether you choose to focus your attention on others or yourself, you are part of this evolving system which encompasses us all. When one part of a system changes, the whole must change with it. Balance is always restored.

Therefore, by developing your own skills, achieving what you want from life and living in pursuit of your true potential, you have an impact which reaches father than you may currently realise. You touch the lives of others in every moment, through the expectations that you create, the experiences you share and the memories you leave behind. And in this you leave something of yourself with everyone who you work with.

Just as you carry around role models of people who have made a real difference in your life – friends, leaders, entertainers, teachers – so you become a role model in other people's lives, and they will forever carry their impression of you with them.

So as you reflect on this part of the journey, these steps that we have taken side by side, you can look back and see how our footprints have mingled and merged, sharing your experiences, your fears and your dreams in order to enrich this learning and growing process.

I want to take this opportunity to thank you for choosing to spend this part of your journey with me and to wish you safe travels ahead as you continue to follow your path and to be open to the new horizons and new possibilities that await you.

¹⁸ Further Reading

18.1   Books

Tricks of the Mind	Derren Brown
Secrets of the Amazing Kreskin	Kreskin
How to Win Friends & Influence People	Dale Carnegie
59 Seconds	Richard Wiseman
Quirkology	Richard Wiseman
The NLP Practitioner Manual	Peter Freeth
The NLP Master Practitioner Manual	Peter Freeth
Change Magic	Peter Freeth
Learning Changes	Peter Freeth
Coaching Excellence	Peter Freeth
NLP – Skills for Learning[13]	Peter Freeth
The Brain that Changes Itself	Normal Doidge
Growing Up With Lucy	Steve Grand

---

13 This is a free download from Bookboon. Just search 'bookboon peter freeth nlp' and you'll find it.

18.2   Websites

My upcoming training dates and other information:

www.nenlp.com

My corporate consulting website:

www.geniuslearning.co.uk

My occasional blog about modelling excellence:

www.genius-at-work.co.uk

On the Brain, a popular neuroscience blog:

merzenich.positscience.com

Scientists use brain imaging to reveal movies in our mind:

news.berkeley.edu/2011/09/22/brain-movies

Principles of Learning, Implications for Teaching:

www.cne.psychol.cam.ac.uk/pdfs/publication-
pdfs/Goswami_JOPE_42_3-4_381-399_2008.pdf

Making long-term memories in minutes: a spaced learning
pattern from memory research in education:

www.ncbi.nlm.nih.gov/pmc/articles/PMC3782739

Keep an Eye on the Time, Neuroscience-based research
makes the case for chunked, spaced learning:

www.td.org/Publications/Magazines/TD/TD-
Archive/2014/01/Keep-An-Eye-on-the-Time

19 The Author

I first encountered NLP in 1993 while working in the Telecoms industry and I've been studying, developing and teaching it ever since. I'm now one of only 6 SNLP licensed Master Trainers in the world, having certified with Christina Hall to the highest level possible.

As the author of such well received books as "NLP in Business", "Change Magic" and "Genius at Work", I have an unparalleled breadth and depth of experience in applying NLP in business to create measurable performance improvements, such as a 700% increase in profitability for a global engineering company.

I've taught NLP all over the world, and have been a "guest trainer" with some of the UK's best known NLP training companies. Today, my focus is on executive coaching and business performance consulting, using a unique talent modelling approach which enables me to replicate high performance within an organisational culture.

I'm an expert in 'modelling' high performers; figuring out the hidden secrets of your highest performers and turning that insight into leadership, management and sales development programs that are perfectly aligned with your culture and business strategy.

My innovative approach has led to:

- 700% increase in profitability for a leading global engineering company

- 25% reduction in graduate development time and cost for a High Street retailer

- 200% increase in sales conversion rates for a contact centre operator

On top of that, I have 15 years L&D experience across all market sectors and organisational levels; leadership and management development, coaching, NLP, sales, business strategy, and another 20 years corporate experience in technology and sales.

If you would like to know more about me, my consultancy business or public speaking opportunities, just get in touch.

Website	www.geniuslearning.co.uk
NLP training	www.nenlp.com
Email	peter@geniuslearning.co.uk
Linkedin	uk.linkedin.com/in/peterfreethgenius
Facebook	www.facebook.com/peter.freeth.genius
Twitter	@genius_learning

19.1.1   Testimonials

"I was fortunate enough to complete the Practitioner course with Peter in 2016 and would recommend his training to anyone who is looking at how they approach the challenges they might face. Peter showed a willingness to learn what each of us on the course wanted to gain and how we might apply new skills. This focus on the real world application of these techniques backed up by the benefit of Peter's experience and pragmatic approach were incredibly valuable and enjoyable. I finished the course eager to revisit my approach to training design and delivery and have since made changes which are increasing learner engagement."

Patrick Armstrong

"Peter's talent for analysing, deconstructing and distilling complex material via anecdotes, metaphor, demos, case parallels and small group practice to enliven the learning, combined with his knack for connecting the dots between course material and our own 'real world' circumstances, has made the experience invaluable for me and is why Peter stands out above the rest."

Cynthia Jacques

"Peter is a coaching genius. I have had several coaching sessions with Peter as well as attending his accredited NLP training courses. Peter is an incisive, focused, challenging and playful coach who has the knack of getting right to the core of an issue quickly and without intrusion. He is hugely inspiring, influential, supporting and caring at the same time. "Time with Peter is an investment that pays back time and time again."

Tony Moorcroft

"15 Years later and I'm still using the techniques Peter taught. I first met Peter when he agreed to speak at one of our conferences. He has an incredible ability to captivate large audiences and still manage to communicate with everyone individually. He always got great feedback. There's no text book to do lists, Peter is able to make it personal, giving real life, useable solutions that are practical and give results immediately. Even when there are irrational fears, such as public speaking. In an hour I was armed with an approach and a state of mind that I still use today."

Simon Polledri

"I had barely heard of NLP before I signed up to Peter's Practitioner course ten years ago. I was extremely fortunate to have him as my trainer and the NLP course was a revelation! NLP has enhanced my own life and my work (teaching, training and career coaching) ever since and I have found his books as entertaining and informative as his training."

Ruth Guy

"Peter is someone who practices what he teaches. He teaches not what is written in a book but real practical stuff. It's fairly simple, you learn and you execute. The process between learning and doing simply unfolds. The false beliefs and limitations I held all my life seemed to disintegrate like magic. And whether you believe in magic or not - attend his training, you will experience a phenomenon that's magic."

Tapas Malaiya

"Having just completed the NLP Master Practitioner in Spain with Peter Freeth, I honestly cannot think of a more fantastic learning experience and I have been on many! This course is about "mastery" not just learning techniques and theory, it is highly interactive and immersive and with constant oversight from Peter I felt supported at all times. Overall, an excellent training experience and a complete shift in many aspects of my own skills and thinking. I cannot recommend this course highly enough."

Steve Heneghan

"Peter Freeth has the rare talent. His training approach engages your brain at a level deeper than mere understanding, he helps you to learn how to teach yourself, to question and challenge your beliefs and perceptions rather than just regurgitating a bunch of information and techniques. His knowledge and experience of using NLP in a business environment is impressive and I have learned a lot from him. I would highly recommend Peter's immersive master practitioner course."

John Lesley

"Peter is a world-class Master Facilitator and has shared his vast experience and insight with many of us. His ability to Coach and understand people behaviour is also commendable. At the same time he remains a keen learner, open for new ideas and concepts with a high level of intercultural sensitivity.

He is one of the best trainers I have seen and worked with. He has the ability to bring out the best in people through putting them at ease. I will strongly recommend Peter for Executive Coaching and Leadership Programs."

Nitin Thakur

"I became General Manager of a Business Development function in a new "intra-penuerial" division. New markets, solutions and team members were all needed. I was looking for support to improve my ability to generate results from and with all these new people, not forgetting my peers in the leadership team and our executives.

Working with Peter gave me techniques which, in many ways used my innate senses, wisdom and abilities to really enhance how I took action. I was able to pace my interactions to those of the individuals and teams I interacted with. Too often our focus on content success, failure and answers confuses our chance to see the other person. Once I was tuned into a client or a team member I could lead with them to the places I needed to us to find together. This really helped developing new business opportunities and it also gave me the tools to be clear and straight forward without complication or conflict. A key strength I gained, through understanding why I was doing this, was the self-belief to stand up and communicate with vision and really lead teams and interactions. Knowing why helps to unearth the natural passion for the challenge and the satisfaction of achieving.

It wasn't all plain sailing, managing and leading never is and the tough issues, exiting poor performers, tricky client situations, tough executive reviews, tense management relationships were all enhanced through my work with Peter.

Peter's support was vital in;

- Helping me recruit 25 new team members and bringing almost all of them to quota,

- In selling £0.3bn in two years, landing milestone deals in a new market and new technology area,

- and in giving our executive confidence in our growth that generated their investment of time and resources."

Guy Wood, Director, Sales Development, CGI (Global IT Services company)

"Peter supported our recent Strategic Management Board away day, looking at our future strategy and vision. His interventions were clear and kept us focussed on the agreed outcomes for the day in an excellent way. He did not shy away from challenging us or giving us some simple tools to bring clarity. We look forward to working with him again in the future."

Matt Prosser, Strategic Director at South Oxfordshire Council

"I enjoyed working with Peter in a mentoring capacity which helped my personal development and confidence to take on a much bigger role. I would recommend working with Peter to support in the training and development arena with you or your teams."

Andrew Pettingill, Managing Director at Meridian Business Support

"Peter is a highly creative and thoughtful coach with an excellent knowledge of his subject. He has a very personable and pragmatic approach that encourages his clients explore their issues."

Stephen Cordell MCIPD, L&D Manager at Parker Hannifin

"Peter Freeth has a unique approach to putting theory into action. I recommend his book to Learning and Development professionals, HR managers or trainers."

Manny Richter, Human Resources Manager, Bostik

"Peter is a quality focussed professional who sets and expects high standards of performance. Peter is able to provide real value to clients and deliver courses and learning of a high quality. The knowledge and experience that Peter has enables him to build relationships well and to inspire others around him to produce their best."

Gavin Muge, Gavin Muge Learning & Development

"I worked closely with Peter Freeth at Oxford Brookes University, and was very impressed by Peter's knowledge of his subject area, and the attention to detail he gave regarding the terms and conditions of the contracts we discussed. I had great confidence that having agreed the terms and conditions of the contracts with Peter, our interests were well protected."

Kevin Henderson, Contracts Manager, Oxford Brookes University

"Peter is highly skilled at building business relationships at all levels. He combines strong commercial awareness with exceptionally clear verbal and written communication. In my experience, Peter always delivers on projects that he is involved in, and I confidently recommend him as a business partner."

Ian Wycherley, Programme Director, Oxford Brookes University

19.1.2 Reviews for Peter's books

"Coaching Excellence - A straightforward, no holds barred guide to the steps to coaching mastery. As well as boiling down the real keys to an effective coaching session, it also explores the behaviours that coaches sometimes have that hold them back from making a real difference. A powerful read from start to finish, and a book that I'm revisiting constantly to help refine my skills and push through the fear, whoever's fear it happens to be."

Matt Hatson

"Hugely practical and refreshingly straight-forward. A must for any coach, teacher or trainer."

David Nicoll

"A practical, congruent and elegant handbook that I can not praise highly enough ... inspiring, stimulating and highly practical"

Stephen Cotterell

"This really is as good as they say"

Karl Tyler

"This is one of the most practical toolkits I have found for opening up thinking and creating new possibilities. One of a leader's 'must have' books"

David Nicoll

"I actually felt that I wasn't reading this book but having a conversation with the author. Peter's style is very much to write to the inner voice, the internal critic that we all have and I found myself answering the questions posed along the way. He has made it a very engaging book indeed - how many books do that now? No doubt you will hear that something is "common sense" without stopping to think what that means. What struck me in this book was that if you want a good idea about what common sense actually looks like in practice, then it's contained within the pages of Change Magic. The principles contained are ideal advice for anybody engaged in change (and who isn't nowadays?) at work, and also to build into training programs which are about personal change or for those who bring it about. I have to say none of this was included in my formal management qualifications but really, it should have been."

Stephen Hopkirk - ESH Associates

"If I had to reduce my business library to one book, this would be it. Peter's approach is practical, down to earth, and perpetually challenging. This chap is to be counted amongst the business gurus/greats. And he has one great advantage over many of them - his stuff actually works across the whole business not just for 'strategy' people."

David Nicoll

"Peter gift wraps startling ideas with great entertainment. Peter has enough intellectual power to make this a 'MUST HAVE BOOK' ...Change Magic has conviction, style, knowledge and humour."

Michael Flaherty, Practice Manager (RAMC) 29 Commando Regt (RA)

"A practical and engaging set of everyday problem solving tools which is guaranteed to generate solutions to problems, and leave users with smiles on their faces. Magic!"

Geoff Cook, MD, The Training Partnership

"A wealth of new insights and ideas, Change Magic represents a different approach so that you can take away your own unique interpretations and apply them into the real world of organisational change."

Peter Harty, MD, Innervision Performance Coaching

"Not just another book about how to think outside the box. No check list or recipes to follow but definitely full of ideas that challenge your established routines and conventional thinking. No matter how successful you have been in the business world, a must read for all. Very inspiring book... should be given to all employees and managers at every level of the organization when they come on board."

Jean-Baptiste Gruet, VP Global Sales, Workplace Options

"Excellent, brilliant, just what I was looking for. The book now looks like I've had it for years and has loads of sticky markers all over it. I've now become more aware and refined, honed and adapted using the suggestions and tips and I've been using/applying it all over the last two weeks with fantastic results. This week however I've had phenomenal reactions from the sales staff in the classroom sessions I've been running. So a very big THANK YOU."

Karen Stockton, Associated New Media

19.2 Other books by Peter Freeth

Also look for The Unsticker on the Google Play Store. It's free, it's world famous, and you'll never be stuck again.

Made in United States
North Haven, CT
20 August 2023

40552777R00176